M000002685

The Toilets of New York

Copyright © 1990 by Ken Eichenbaum

All rights reserved under International and Pan American Copyright Conventions.

Published in the United States by *LITTERATI BOOKS,*
4100 West River Lane, Milwaukee, Wisconsin USA 53217.
Telephone 414 354-5441.

No maps, illustrations, or other portions of this book may be reproduced in any form without written permission from the publisher.

ISBN NO. 0-9620271-2-X

The Toilets of New York

A HANDY GUIDE TO THE BEST (AND THE WORST)
PUBLIC AND SEMIPUBLIC RELIEF STATIONS
FOR THOSE WITH A NEED-TO-KNOW.
INCLUDES WALKING AND TROTTING MAPS.

BY KEN EICHENBAUM

"What this country needs is a chicken in every pot, a toilet in every house, and a good five-cent cigar.**"**

**VICE PRESIDENT ANDREW H. HIGGINS
IN A SPEECH BEFORE CONGRESS, 1824**

"No citizen, regardless of age, should be deprived of the comfort and convenience of a well-appointed, indoor lavatory, with plenty of quality roll-goods.**"**

**LADY ESTELLE HAWKS, CHAIRWOMAN
AMALGAMATED PAPER AND PULP, LTD.**

"A hundred years from now, people will relieve themselves in small, tiled, private chambers connected by pipes to a water supply, and artificially illuminated by glowing transparent globes screwed in brass sockets.**"**

**KENDALL G. PARQUETTE
IN A PAPER DELIVERED BEFORE THE
N.Y. SANITARIA DIRECTORS LAST MONTH**

"Hey! Where you going, buddy? If you're not eating here you're not using that john. Buzz off, and take the whimpering kid with you.**"**

**FARLEY QUIMBLE
WAITER AND PART OWNER OF
THE FOOT O'SWINE DINER, E. 39TH ST.**

For **CATE CHARLTON,** without whose constant need to search out the nearest toilet facilities on a visit to New York, the idea for this book might never have seen the light of day...

And for **JANE JARVIS,** without whose keyboard magic at the PC, the handwritten scrawls of the harried researchers might never have seen the clarity of print...

And for **TODD EICHENBAUM,** without whose intimate, first-hand knowledge of spelling and SoHo restaurants, the accuracy of this guidebook might always be in question...

And, for **THE PEOPLE OF NEW YORK,** the maitre d's and washroom attendants, the police persons and coffee shop cashiers, the desk clerks and box office workers, without whose patient collaboration this data might never have been acquired.

TABLE OF CONTENTS

INTRODUCTION

There is a story about a gentleman from Milwaukee who attends a seminar in New York. Having never visited the city before, he decides to stay on for a couple of days to do some sightseeing. So, for 48 hours he scurries about the city, taking in Times Square, Lincoln Center, several museums, the United Nations Building, the theatre district, and Rockefeller Center. Then, just as he prepares to leave for the airport, he realizes he has not yet seen the Empire State Building. Quickly, he steps outside the hotel and stops a man on the sidewalk. "Excuse me, sir," he says, "but can you tell me how to get to the Empire State Building, or should I go screw myself?"

That is a true story. It is living testimony to the indisputable fact that New Yorkers are a separate breed. They can be friendly or fierce, condescending or caustic, ugly or pleasant. And that's just one New Yorker.

Behavioral psychologists tell us that is because New Yorkers live on top of one another. In North Dakota, for example, they don't stack residents. They measure their populations by the number of people per acre. In such a sparse environment, folks are genuinely pleased to see one another. Human encounters are serendipitous. In

Manhattan, populations are gauged by the number of persons per cubic yard. One is never more than three feet from another human being. More often, you are shoulder to shoulder with pickpockets, Pakistanis, gay rights activists, and Japanese businessmen. Language is not the primary barrier. Noise is. To make yourself understood above the pandemonium, a visitor must cultivate a high piercing shriek. Broad hand and arm gestures will help, too.

Those who cannot suppress a well-mannered childhood (where one opens doors for senior citizens, and moderated speech is admired) will find it difficult to communicate in New York. Fluency in Durhan or Japanese will help, but not a lot.

Locating a toilet under these conditions thus becomes a major undertaking. The situation is exacerbated in direct proportion to need. If you ask a person on the street, the odds are three to five you'll be talking to someone who arrived yesterday from Denver. If you ask a taxi driver, the odds are eight to ten his English is confined to meter-reading, the names of three or four major hotels, and anything with the word "trump" in it. Unless there is a Trump Toilet, the term "wash room" is not in his vernacular. If you ask a cop, and if he pauses long enough to hear your question, he will be blunt. The odds are seven to ten a seasoned member of New York's finest will respond with "Heyclown, yakidn? Drayntnun rond heeya!"

It is not a healthy situation. Many visitors have taken to wearing devices made for the incontinent. Yet, these still require frequent return trips to the hotel, and an uneasy housekeeping staff. The need for a toilet guidebook is obvious.

CHAPTER 1: METHODOLOGY

In New York, among those who have the need to relieve themselves, men have fewer obstacles than women. Internists, knowledgeable about such matters, tell us that a man's bladder is twenty-one percent larger, by body-weight, than a woman's corresponding organ. That means men can go for 60 to 80 minutes longer without going. And other physicians tell us that the male liquid waste dispensing system is easier to handle. Moreover, males are usually clad in apparel that requires less maneuvering to gain adequate egress. Like horses, they can accomplish at least half of their waste control measures while in a stand-up position.

Women, on the other hand, are the victims of their own fashion and physiology. Modesty demands they repair to some remote corner, and that they do it an hour sooner. Children and solid waste present two more problems. If the children are very young, they may come equipped with their own disposable holding systems. But older children aren't as fortunate. For this reason, travel agents suggest that they be well fed and watered before the trip, and then re-nourished no more than once a day during the trip, preferably after nightfall.

Of course there are many New York toilets open to the public. But they are not for travelers on a limited budget. The citizens' toilets in Lincoln Center, for example, are marvelously appointed, but tickets to Tosca can run thirty to forty dollars. There are separate lavatories for men and women at the Russian Tea Room, but veal rolled in cabbage leaves can cost upwards of thirty dollars, including a bowl of borscht, a good glass of wine, and strong tea, which won't help matters. Those who are accustomed to slipping into a gas station back home for quick relief will be astonished to discover that there are no gas stations in Manhattan. It is widely believed that most New Yorkers who still drive their own cars order their fuel from a catalog.[1]

All these conditions merely underscore the need for a lavatory guidebook. More than three years of research went into the preparation of this one. But three years is a long time, especially in New York. *We can no longer vouch for the accuracy of our data.* The rapid pace of metropolitan living accelerates the entrepreneurial changes. While Dubuque or Waukegan may have businesses managed by third and fourth generations, in New York some of the bars, clubs and restaurants change ownership almost as often as they change

[1] People who move from the hinterlands to New York often arrive in their automobiles, vans, or pick-up trucks only to discover that indoor parking spaces are harder to find than toilets. When a space is found, it is usually larger and more costly than one's apartment, which has created a brisk business in used cars and automotive parts.

tablecloths. Commercial enterprises that existed 12 months ago—and welcomed needy visitors—may already have been replaced by managements less sympathetic to nature's call.

Why the delays in research? Simple. They were the result of two phenomena that editors could not have anticipated. First of all, in order to generate accurate data, we gave detailed questionnaires to our first group of researchers and asked them not to disclose their true aim. They simply posed as visitors, inquiring about the toilet facilities. We later discovered that some of them found it embarrassing to go from door to door, asking to use the bathroom, when in fact they had no need to use the bathroom. Weeks went by, and only a few reports were sent back to Toilet Central.

Attempts to re-contact the errant researchers proved futile. They vanished and left no forwarding address. Others were hired, this time adequately screened for their ability to ask for the location of a toilet without needing one. But they too slipped into oblivion. It turns out that these persons were unable to cope with rejection.

A whole year had transpired, and yet, less than ten percent of the city had been accurately surveyed.

A strategy meeting of the editorial board was convened. After some debate, it was decided that unemployed actors, writers, and dancers would be the most likely candidates to complete the project. It was reasoned that these persons could assume the personality of one in need of a toilet and, true to their career aspirations, they could also accept rejection and, undaunted, move on to the next establishment.

A cast of 24 was hired and put to work. Only one drawback (a minor one, to be sure) was apparent: the length of the reports they filed. The editors gave each investigator a revised map and simplified questionnaires to complete. At the bottom of each was room for 20 or 30 words of personal observations. Regrettably, some researchers, answering the call of their toilet muse, unbridled their creativity. Descriptions became excessive. In one case, an erstwhile screenwriter composed four illuminating pages on the decor of a particularly impressive men's room.

Another year passed.

Once the final reports came in, the editors had to make a quick decision: re-examine toilets that were toured 24 months earlier, or get the book to market. One might say nature took its course. A few of the more important locations were updated, and the results were put to press.

CHAPTER 2:
AN HISTORICAL
PERSPECTIVE

The history of toilets is fraught with genius, deceit, heroism and treachery. Nowhere is this brought into clearer focus than in the book of Sir Clifford Charlton John's entitled *"Toilets and Treason"*[1]. Dubbed "The John Book" by serious students of the lavatory, Sir Clifford writes in 1791, "He who owns the plumbing controls the throne."

This was no idle boast. Two thousand years B.W.C. the Romans built huge stone aqueducts slanting from their shtetles to the Tigris, not to have a cold drink (as many of today's historians still insist) but to provide a swift system for waste removal. Until that time, clay vessels were used, which were often heavy and cumbersome. Some leaked. The fastest way to lose a good slave was to put her in charge of the waste jars.

1 An account of Sir Clifford's later life relates his fateful voyage to the New World. He set sail from Luton Bedfordshire in the spring of 1803, and died six months later of an exploding bowel in front of The Plaza.

But the history of toilets goes back even further than the Roman aqueduct. In Lascouxe, France, explorers found cave drawings *(Fig. 1)* that clearly depict the primitive lavatory systems then in use.

Later, in a dark corner of Egypt, archaeologists wearing wet handkerchiefs around their faces, unearthed huge, wide-mouthed clay pots which were covered with decorated lids into

Fig. 1 Cave drawings in Lascouxe, France, clearly depict the primitive lavatory systems then in use. Seats were of carved and polished stone, and were apparently part of early man's hunting, eating, sitting cycle.

which small holes had been cut. Dr. Krimin M. Palusch of the Metropolitan Museum[2] was able to

2 Later, Dr. Palusch was to end his professional career in ignominy when Museum Police discovered Egyptian artifacts installed in his own condo's bathroom. After serving six years in an upstate prison, Palusch moved to Hollywood, where major studios were pandering to popular interest in ancient Egypt. He was made technical director of several motion pictures, the most noteworthy of which was "A Mummy For Every Daddy", Warner Brothers, 1933.

decipher their intricate hieroglyphic patterns. His work demonstrated beyond a doubt that these devices were designed to serve but one function *(Fig. 2)*. People were obviously quite smaller in those days.

King Toot Annal Kannal's burial vault *(Fig. 3)* is replete with an adjacent tile bath. It contained nine of these sturdy vessels. According to Dr. Palusch, these were "...to provide the King and his entourage with all the personal conveniences on their dark spiritual journey, even if another attack of dysentery should occur along

Fig. 2 Toilets in early Egypt, pre-dating by centuries the modern commode, demonstrate the innovative thinking of the ancient Royal Waste Control person.

Fig. 3 The burial vault of King Toot Annal Kannal, showing tile bath and nine ceremonial vessels.

the way." Three smaller, less sumptuous baths, may also be seen. These were for the king's wife, his concubine, her lover, and his paramour, all of whom were ceremoniously laid to rest with their dead leader. Hence the term "rest room."

During the reign of Hsing Hsui *(Fig. 4)* in the Dung Dynasty, the emperor, hard pressed for revenue enhancements, sent his representatives to the far corners of the provinces to take a census and levy a tax on each toilet. It was during this period that wealthy, unscrupulous Chinese disguised their bathrooms to look like drawing rooms by upholstering the jade commode and arranging intricately embroidered pillows in the shower stall. Thus, the toilet, which had flourished for centuries before Dung, was lost to the devious strategy of enterprising tax dodgers. It would be centuries before the toilet would emerge from its camouflage to regain its upright position in the home.

In Denmark, a seaman named Lars "The Timid" Hedt was called before his master for refusing to embark on a voyage with his countrymen in the year 1036. Asked to explain his

Fig. 4
Emperor Hsing Hsui (Dung Dynasty) angered over his people's successful efforts to camouflage their toilets after he levied the world's first recorded head tax.

reluctance, Lars said it was basically because, in their haste to float a formidable armada, the Viking craft often had to be christened and launched before they were completed. Thus, the vessels were rarely outfitted with toilets.[3]

Not that all the boats were devoid of creature comforts. According to preserved Viking quartermaster reports, there was often plenty of fresh water, hand soap, toilet tissue, and lamb jerky, bulls apparently being too heavy to jerk in those days. But there were no toilets. In the oral history of Denmark, scholars report Lars' battle cry was, "I won't go if I can't go."

This displeased the captain as well as the seaman's wife. Mrs. "The Timid" Hedt, in order to get her husband out of the house, besought the royal boat builders and pleaded with them to retrofit a toilet onto at least one of the vessels. They agreed. To this day, any person on board any seagoing craft in the world, wishing to relieve him/herself will announce, "I'm going to the Hedt."

Eastern European culture is spotted with similar toiletry episodes. The Russians, for example, loathe being regarded as primitive or unsophisticated. This attitude goes back to the days of Czar Hullotzckeh the Second, who gave a loyal subject named Nyod Goodinov Paskudnyak "...all

3 On an earlier excursion, "The Timid" was horribly disfigured while seated on the rail of his boat, in the act of relieving himself. The Viking craft was sideswiped in mid- Atlantic by another vessel, sliding Lars 16 feet along the rail. Both the ship's carpenter and cook were called on deck to administer first aid. They removed splinters and applied rancid Scandinavian butter to the wounds. It would be months before "The Timid" could even venture near the sea again without shivering his haunches and developing a cold sweat.

the lands north of the Volga, bounded on the east by Horsnograd, on the west by the old Kapoolia Road, and on the north by the Arctic Circle."

Nyod Goodinov *(Fig. 5)* went by troika to his fiefdom in March of that year. By May, the odor was so bad he was back in Moscow, standing in his soiled garments before the Czar. There were no waste facilities that far north, he complained. What was more, the frost line went down

Fig. 5 Nyod Goodinov Paskudnyak was rewarded by the Czar for his loyalty and the neat way he trimmed his beard. But by the time of the summer thaw, a problem with the peasants emerged.

60 feet in some areas. So, all winter the peasants simply emptied their steaming vessels into the snow out back. It was a natural deep freeze. But when the spring thaw arrived, the atmosphere became unbearable.

The Czar, who had a cold, couldn't care less. But the Czarina *(Fig. 6)*, whose nasal passages were clear, took pity on her subject, saying, "Nyod Goodinov Paskudnyak, here is a chest filled with one million rubles and a hundred rolls of paper. Go back to your lands and construct a communal toilet. But, please, leave now."[4]

In parts of England and Scotland, the chamber pot still persists, not due to a dearth of mechanical ingenuity so much as to the overwhelming British urge to retain certain traditions. Even some of the fancier hotels have eschewed modern plumbing in favor of the bed vessel, much to the chagrin of visiting Americans, who must often wake early and take themselves across the road to a McDonald's.

The history of the toilet in America is far more colorful than elsewhere in the world. We are a young nation. Our toilets are a melting pot, if you will, of many diverse cultures, each with its own hopes and dreams, each with its own vision of what a good toilet should be.

---

4 This is the first record of a public W.C. in Russia, and its simple design has remained unchanged in well over two centuries.

Fig. 6 The Czarina immediately recognized Paskudnyak's difficulties and took swift steps to help him correct conditions with money and supplies. To this day she is mentioned in prayers and literature, and in Ballaboostok there is an inlaid toilet seat with her name on it.

The Pilgrims, on their first visit to Plymouth's rocky shores, brought with them toilet seats of scrimshaw, delicately incised with nautical scenes *(Fig. 7)*. These etchings were neatly transferred, albeit in reverse, to those early Americans'

Fig. 7 A section of an early American nautical toilet seat, carved from whale bone, and incised with delicate scenes that left their mark on seamen.

hindquarters. Having no television, the newcomers would often moon each other around the campfire, pointing out scenes they recognized, or whales who looked familiar.

The native American Indians were intrigued by the settlers' designs, and—friendly as they were—inaugurated one of the earliest cultural exchanges on record. They showed the colonists how to fashion seats from birch bark, and pull-chains from carved buffalo teeth.[5] America was on its way, sanitarily speaking.

In New York, just before the turn of the century, engineers planning the world's most spectacular underground transportation system, got their heads together, so to speak, and decided to install modern lavatory facilities in every subway station. At first, water from the East River was to be used for flushing, but it was too thick for the pipes. Unfortunately, the contract for extra heavy commodes had already been let, and it could not be canceled. Hydroengineers hunted around until they discovered less viscous waters under some nearby meadows (later called Flushing Meadows) and work proceeded.

Early construction records reveal that fourteen brave workers lost their lives trying to position the heavy commodes in those dim underground passageways. One man, Pheeny O'Rourke[6], was a

---

5 In the hunter-gatherer societies, toiletry requirements change with the seasons. In the summer, for example, some tribes dispensed with seats and other accoutrements, opting for a secluded glen and a handful of eucalyptus leaves.

6 Pheeny was not considered a reliable source. A journalist, working on the *Times* story, said his speech was slurred, his eyes bleary, and he staggered when he walked. At first this was attributed to his line of work. Ten hours in an underground toilet often afflicted news reporters with identical symptoms.

foreman on that project and, in a *New York Times* Sunday magazine article dated September 19, 1891, he was quoted as saying, "They'll ne'er appreciate our sacrifice, those friggin' commuters."

Perhaps. But, Mr. O'Rourke, if he were alive today, would be astonished to learn that, of the original 3657 subway toilets he and his co-workers installed, 1144 have already been closed, either for dis-use or misuse. Each year, a few more subterranean lavatories are drained and sealed.

City fathers claim the closings have saved New York taxpayers over $3 million a year in cleaning labor, toilet paper, and that foul-smelling liquid soap that never foams.

Municipal cost controls are admirable, but no one can measure the resultant anguish in dollars. A few years ago, when the city was on the verge of bankruptcy, a councilman moved that, rather than sealing up more restrooms, silver dollar coin devices be placed on the remaining stalls. The response was immediate. An angry populace, led by pacifist Abdullah Ponjokopur[7], had to be dragged from the tiled subway floors by special police squads. Needless to say, the coin meters were quickly removed, and a bond issue was underwritten by Congress.

---

[7] Not his real name. Ponjokopur, *a.k.a.* Punjab the Spirit, it was later revealed, was the name adopted by Tyrone "The Flush" Kelly, a Brooklyn resident who often used his charismatic skills and other aliasi to lobby for various causes. After the toilet incident, he assumed the name of Ralph Grundy and campaigned for free restaurant meals. This time vigilant police who were wise to his strategy arrested him and his band of free-meal followers in the fourth floor restaurant of Bloomingdale's, where they were trying to make off with trays of ketchup, marmalade, and ice water.

New York is not alone. In Paris, once known as the city of pissoirs, similar changes were occurring. Workmen, usually in the dead of night to avoid confrontations, unbolted and removed these circular sidewalk toilets. They were regarded as a nuisance by the Ministry of Health and Commerce.

For years after their removal, angry Frenchmen defied the law and continued to use the places where the pissoirs once stood, shouting *"Fraternite, Uranite, Egality!"* while raising only one fist. Today, other than for a few rust stains on the concrete walkways, there is little to remind the strolling tourist of that romantic period in French history when one could relieve himself on nearly any street corner.[8]

I n Budapest, residents could always count on the public facilities early settlers had installed on barges that were anchored in the river that divided the city. Next to every important bridge that crossed the river, there were steps that led down to the moorings. In one hop you could be piped aboard a toilet barge and be on your way again. But soon the business community prevailed on the Budapest city council. They insisted that the barges impeded river traffic and hindered com-

---

8 There was little consideration for the distaff population in France even then. Unless a woman worked in the chorus line at the Moulin Rouge or sang in a cabaret, her toilet requirements went virtually unheeded.

merce. So, on one night in 1902 *(Schtunkenacht)* municipal employees, moving silently and quickly, poured petrol *(Fig. 8)* on all eleven barges and set them ablaze.[9]

The results were more than the business leaders could have predicted. True, from that

Fig. 8 The fiery scene in Budapest on the night employees set fire to the municipal toilet barges anchored in the river. Eleven barges were sent to the bottom (a reversal of prior events, so to speak).

time forward, residents and visitors would have to rely on the hospitality of innkeepers and restaurateurs, which increased trade. But this one act, perhaps more than any other, galvanized political action against the community's capitalists and

9 At one time, the very river that inspired Beethovan to compose his now familiar Blue Danube Waltz, was so clear one could actually make out the empty mit-schlag cans on the sandy bottom. At dawn following *Schtunkenacht*, the entire armada of Budapest's floating conveniences lay charred beneath the waves, and to this day, tales of the murky water are used to frighten bed-wetting Hungarian children.

their bureaucratic lackeys, and (as we know now) did more than anything else to open the door to Communism.

No history of toilets would be complete without mentioning those hearty inhabitants of the Antarctic who daily brave the elements in the discharge of their toiletary obligations. The environment is cruel. Temperatures frequently drop to 200 degrees below zero. Under those conditions, refrigerators or freezers are useless. They heat up their contents. Milk left on the doorstep

Fig. 9 Commander Sven Molsnen, the noted Swedish explorer, came back from the Antarctic with glowing reports of communal toilets with ermine-lined seats.

gets brittle. Spit out your chewing gum and it becomes a deadly missile. Skin left exposed for more than 40 seconds can be kissed goodbye. And infants are always in an ugly mood because they are forced to drink brittle milk.

Just before the turn of the century, explorers under the leadership of Commander Sven Molsnen *(Fig. 9)* were astonished to find thousands of friendly, fur-clad natives happily living under these conditions. Sven writes, in his *Antarctic Travels of the Gay Nineties*, "Several members of each tribe are designated *'No Nik Ko Mode Chik Nook'*, or ice sculptors. Their responsibility is to keep the communal ice toilets in constant repair. Just as we [in Sweden] have been warned not to place our tongues on pump handles, their culture cautions against sitting on a freshly carved seat. By our standards, they have luxurious facilities, lined with real fur and frequently padded with ermine. O'Malley and Runkel, our American team members, showed them picture postcards of Fort Lauderdale and Daytona Beach. The beggars had never seen palm trees or sand before, or women out of their grizzly suits. Within a week, half the members of the tribe were last seen heading north, which is the only way you can go if you're in the South Pole."

CHAPTER 3:
A GOOD TOILET
IS HARD TO FIND

O ver the years, the results of the mass world-wide shutdown of public conveniences has taken its toll on the urban dweller and the traveler. Meanwhile, back in the U.S., other events took place that would have equally devastating effects on the collective American bladder and bowel.

On a spring day in 1933, unbeknownst to the public at large, representatives of the nation's leading architectural firms met with builders and developers *(Fig. 10)* at a small resort hotel just outside Las Vegas, Nevada. They arrived by bus, private jet and stretch limo. To the casual observer, nothing seemed amiss. They appeared like any other Vegas executives; pinstriped suits with wide lapels, broad-brimmed hats, silk shirts with flowered ties, large silk pocket squares, and pointed lizard-skin shoes. Dressed this way, they escaped detection by the local press.

The architects had a secret agenda. Their plan was to revolutionize the American skyscraper.

That tall symbol of America's standard of living was to be altered in a number of devious ways.

It would take decades before their ideas would be fully implemented, but that did not deter them from their mission. *First*, the architects

Fig. 10 Architects and real estate developers convening in Las Vegas during the early thirties, to set down design and construction guidelines for the installation of concealed toilets in public buildings such as hotels and skyscrapers.

agreed that, at every opportunity, they would convince developer-owners that neo gothic was the only route to go; that there should be pillars and peaked roofs, arches and brick. *Second,* that the first floor should always be elevated 30 to 40 feet to provide a so-called "public plaza" at ground level for pedestrians. (They chuckled at this term, knowing that there would be absolutely no lavatories at ground level; that, in fact, the only conveniences would be virtually inaccessible by anyone but a tenant with set of keys to the building).

A subcommittee of this group devoted their attention specifically to hotels and restaurants. They too drew up a list of architectural non-amenities which included hiding toilet facilities either in a sub basement, or on a mezzanine that could only be reached by a narrow, winding stairway, or with a block and tackle.

In addition, they compiled a carefully worded document that contained a list of vocal responses for hotel managers and maitre d's to use when asked, "Where is your toilet?" This list contains such phrases as: "Madame, are you a guest here?" "Sir, we have no public toilets"; "I'm sorry, but the toilet is being remodeled. Will you be dining with us today?" and, most vicious of all, a response in some foreign tongue, such as Gaelic, to avoid any further inquiries.

Another ploy is to place a small sign on a tripod in front of the toilet that reads "Wet Floor" or "Out of Service, Use Toilet in Next Building."

If you were to query a senior partner at any major U.S. architectural firm today he would feign ignorance of that fateful Las Vegas meeting. Yet, evidence of their collusion is unmistakable.

The only way we were able to get wind of it was through a disgruntled maitre d' *(Fig. 11)* who was summarily dismissed by one of Manhattan's most

Fig. 11 We met Deep Toilet late one night in a riverfront telephone booth where, in exchange for a five-dollar bill, the former maitre d' allowed us to examine his copy of *Responses to Tourists' Toilet Inquiries*. It is filled with deception, misdirection, and hypocrisy. It will be the subject of a docudrama on HBO late next year.

prestigious restaurants for showing his ailing mother, not a customer, to the women's room.

The fearful results of such willful abuse by architects and developers can be witnessed first hand on any day by any visitor to New York. Finding a toilet is a grueling experience.

As a fellow tourist, we are pleased to report that we do have some recourse. Inaccessibility to toilets should not deter you from visiting this fascinating metropolis. New York is a marvel of sights and sounds. For the walker who wishes to explore every corner, every store window and every shop, the city is unequaled among the capitols of the world. It offers the bustle of London, the romanticism of Paris, the diversity of Rome, the glamour of San Francisco. But, thank heaven, it does not offer the drinking water of Mexico City.

What is the future of toilets? The question stirs the souls of every man, woman and child in this hemisphere and others. Why? Because, for too long, most of the emphasis has been on hydraulic engineering, not on accessibility.

If this condition should change, it will probably happen first in buildings designed for governmental use. Why? Because Unequal Rights Workers are already lobbying state legislatures. Lawmakers are beginning to realize the fundamental differences between men and women. Egalitarianism may be okay when it comes to equal pay for equal work. But on-site research demonstrates that women need twice as many toilets as men because they take twice as long to use them.

Fig. 12 This mild, unassuming associate professor at the Grenada Architectural College is Dr. Fletcher Owen Commode, a toilet fighter who believes that equality between the sexes ends at the threshold of the lavatory. He is shown with the 1990 Golden Roll award, an honor bestowed upon him by the Society to Help Improve Toilets.

The forces of democratic action have already begun to alter the status quo. One might call this new movement the broken winds of change.

Once the legislators become enlightened, building codes will change, and architects will have to conform to the new requirements. The strategy is long overdue. We are indebted to activitists like Dr. Fletcher Owen Commode *(Fig. 12)* and his small band of embattled lobbyists who have given compelling testimony before several state planning commissions. Others are getting behind them. With luck, by the year 2000, all new, publicly-funded structures will be user friendly.

CHAPTER 4: SOME TRAVEL OBSERVATIONS

If you are entering New York via one of the airports (LaGuardia, Kennedy International, Newark) visit the toilet before boarding land-transport to the city. A traffic jam could keep you taxi bound for an hour. If you're driving to New York, don't. But if you must, there are three things you can do with your car: (1) leave it in the suburbs and take a cab, (2) park it in your hotel garage, then arrange for a second mortgage on your home to reclaim it, or (3) simply park it on the street. It will be silently and efficiently dismantled, with all parts removed before daybreak.

If man is a social animal, then cities are the tangible result of his needs. Bigger cities become both better and worse with their growth. London, Tokyo, Rio de Janeiro and New York share this good/bad phenomenon, but new York has an edge on the others, perhaps because it is more concentrated (more wealth, more poverty, more people, more ideas, more artists, more visitors, more beauty, more trash, all closer together).

So, as you move about the city, remain tolerant. These little walking maps are merely jump-starts to self-conducted excursions that may carry you on foot to adventures that a hundred years ago could only be imagined by Earth's most feverish, wealthy, and unbalanced inhabitants.

On the pages that follow are a number of walking (or trotting) tours. Each has certain attributes to recommend it, depending on your physical state, the amount of time at your disposal, and the condition of the weather or your traveling companion.

Unlike some travel books, these pedestrian tours are not designed by *topic* so much as they *are by area*, with the assumption that—if you're on a walking tour—you don't want to take a taxi between sites. So, instead, we've taken sections of Manhattan that vary from ten to twenty square blocks, point out various buildings, shops, and other points of interest, and list those places where you can most likely find a toilet.

Whenever possible, the toilets are rated. Information regarding wheelchair access, lighting, number of stalls, and the general quality of the facilities is listed. In larger buildings, their location may also be designated.

Medical research has revealed that many travelers will often calculate the length of their walk based on an equation that factors in the distance between facilities. For these persons, the walking maps will be an invaluable aid.

HOW TO USE THE MAPS

Adjacent to each walking map is a miniature schematic drawing to enable you to see the map's relationship to the rest of the city. Major streets, Central Park, and other features will help you become better oriented.

Just one more word about maps and orientation: we know that, like us, some folks panic when they're confronted with anything that even *resembles* a map. Maps could be printed in Sikh or Celanese for all the help they are to those pitiful individuals. All they see are criss-cross lines running into other lines. Non-map-reading people will be delighted to see that each of our walking maps (shall we call them diagrams, to help allay your juvenile fear of losing your mother again?)... has a star and a dotted line.

With the help of a hotel concierge, a cop, or (if you're lucky) a fellow pedestrian who speaks English, try to get to the place on the ground represented by that star. Once you get there, proceed along the dotted line. (Remember: the dotted line will *not* be visible on the sidewalk, only on your diagram.) Walk along until you pass the first street shown on your diagram. If it says (for example) Houston St. on a street sign in front of you, and the same words appear on the map, voila! You're using the right map.

Just keep trying to pass any one of the streets shown along the dotted line. If you do that, on some maps you should wind up back at the star where you started. If you should lose your way, simply drop us a postcard and we will notify a New York City Mounted Policeman, who will be delighted to share his saddle and two pounds of oats with you, if you don't mind eating out of a canvas bag.

Here, then, are some walking tours of this majestic urban adventure. Major sites are clearly identified, although (as previously explained) the dynamics of the cityscape may already have altered the configuration. Some buildings or enterprises have already been removed and replaced with others. But these changes should be swiftly discernible to the adventurer on foot.

In the great guidebooks of Europe, the editors are quick to advise that a 5-star restaurant, at the time of printing, may already have lost its head chef to another establishment, and disillusioned diners will come away from the table choking and holding their throats. It is with this in mind that we respectfully caution readers that a toilet heretofore described as highly prized for its accessibility, cleanliness, charm, or decor, may now have a sign in front of it that reads "Plumbing Backed Up, Remove Shoes Before Entering."

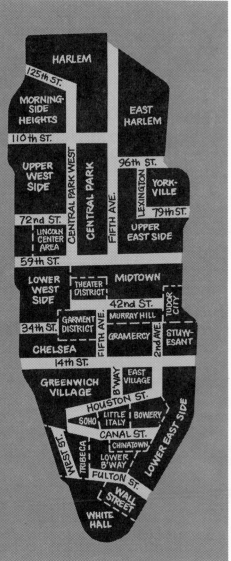

The island of Manhattan is a conglomerate of neighborhoods. Each has its own name. In this diagram (left) you can pick out the major delineating thoroughfares as well as Central Park, which is perhaps the city's most ideal landmark because of its size, location, and grass.

Study this map. When you get home, use terms like "Lower West Side", "Gramercy" and "East Harlem." It will give relatives the notion that you really know New York. You will not fool the natives because they pronounce these names differently. A book on the New York language (with a pronunciation guide) is soon to be published. Watch for it. It's called *Hoddatawkafokes Inna Bigappo Widdott Screwnup.*

AREA A: ROCKEFELLER CENTER

POINTS OF INTEREST

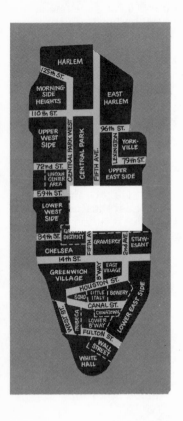

1. UNITED NATIONS Here's where all the international action is. Just browse, or take a guided tour.

2. CHRYSLER BUILDING For one year (1930-31) lauded as the world's tallest building. Neat art deco top.

3. GRAND CENTRAL STATION Crossroads of a million private lives, but a lousy place to seek relief.

4. N.Y. PUBLIC LIBRARY You can't withdraw a single volume, but a visit will be fascinating.

5. THE EMPIRE STATE BUILDING An option if your feet can take it. (Sears Tower is taller.)

6. THE DIAMOND CENTER A concentrated block-long array of glittering gold and shiny jewelers.

7. ROCKEFELLER CENTER A vertical city installed in an impressive cluster of skyscrapers. Check out the fellow with the globe on his back.

8. RADIO CITY MUSIC HALL Houses the world's largest indoor theatre, and a platoon of leggy dancers.

9. SAKS FIFTH AVENUE Floor after floor, this is the shopping experience in its most civilized form.

Find other points of interest (and extraordinarily detailed toilet reports) on the pages that follow.

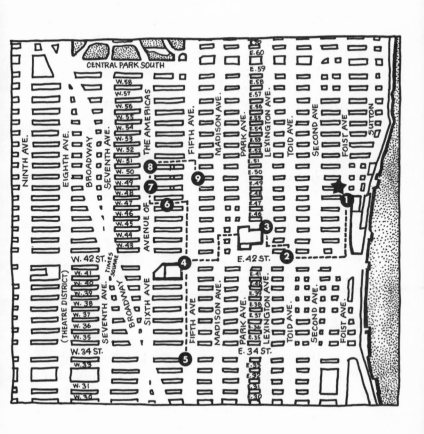

RADIO CITY MUSIC HALL

The world is populated by 5.2 billion souls. A good share of this number may be seen on any day, good weather or bad, waiting in line for tickets to some pageant to be mounted on this, the stage of the largest indoor theatre in the world. The fact that one can write ahead for tickets, or call toll free 1-800 682-8080, does not seem to faze those standing mutely in single file. They are the shuffling dead. Perhaps they feel it is a rite of passage; some ceremony that must be endured before they can be deemed worthy to occupy one of the 6000 seats. There are other favorable factors that deserve attention: Radio City Music Hall—large as it is—has no supporting posts to obscure the audience's vision; the architecture is a textbook example of art deco, preserved by owners with an historical perspective; the Radio City Rockettes provide well-paid jobs for dozens of long-legged dancing girls fresh in from the farms and villages of Iowa, Indiana, North Carolina, and South Dakota, with an opportunity to meet and know wealthy and generous men, and be rewarded for several hours of daily or nightly aerobics. Like any good theatre, the lavatories are well equipped. But take our advice: they are best visited *during* the spectacle, because at intermission the people who were standing outside reform their lines inside, divided by gender.

ROCKEFELLER CENTER

A new, second generation of Americans live and work, as their parents did, in Rockefeller Center. They have seen neither the light of day nor breathed unconditioned air. That is because this enormous complex of 21 skyscrapers is actually a city within a city, with 30 restaurants, several drugstores, shoe repair shops, clothing stores, dentists, hairdressers, banks, a post office, massage parlors, theatres, and chiropractors. It is unnecessary to leave Rockefeller Center, provided your rent is paid. It is where the sovereign nations of Malthus, Labontia, Movoota, and Shera have their consulates, even though their boundaries no longer appear on any map. Representatives of these countries continue to receive massive U.S. aid. During the day, nearly a quarter of a million white-collar types occupy these structures. The buildings are connected underground by a two-mile shopping concourse that would satiate the stoutest potentate. Recently, New Yorkers were horrified to learn that the company that owned Rockefeller Center sold controlling interest in this American shrine to some Japanese, who, it was rumored, were going to rip out the U.S. style toilets and replace them with traditional Asian facilities. This will require fancier footwork. At press time no reconstruction had yet commenced.

NEW YORK PUBLIC LIBRARY

This imposing structure, with its 35 steps rising to great, two-story-high bronze doors, flanked by gigantic stone lions and opening onto a marble-lined hall that could easily accommodate a Big Ten football contest, was apparently designed to frighten citizens into literacy. It works. The New York Public Library on Fifth Avenue is, in fact, a tri-part merger of the city's Astor, Lenox and Tilden libraries, with half the construction costs donated by Andrew Carnegie. More than just a dusty repository for books (there are over five million volumes here), this Library also houses manuscript collections, rare books and maps, special subject departments, galleries, exhibit halls, auditoriums, and a reading room that can seat 550 avid researchers in relative silence. No books or materials can be drawn from this library; they may only be used on the premises. Some departments are open only to those working on a doctorate, or who can prove they do not have greasy fingers. A sophisticated search-and-find computer can locate and produce any book in minutes. Even though the structure was built on the site of the old city reservoir and a paupers' cemetery, it neither is haunted nor has a wet basement. The lions at the entrance have been named "Quiet" and "Please" by the New York State Librarians Association.

GRAND CENTRAL STATION

During more innocent times, nations would compete with each other on the size of their clocks, the populations of their cities, the depth of their lakes. The clock at Grand Central Station, at twelve feet in diameter, is the world's largest indoor timepiece. It has to be that big because it's in a concourse with a 150 foot ceiling (that's about 15 stories high). Anything less would be unworthy. The best angle from which to observe this mighty terminal is up the marble steps to the marble balcony where you'll have an unimpeded view of the melting pot scurrying to and from trains. While you're up there, check out the star-strewn ceiling with its painted winter Zodiac.

Then when you've had your fill of people and marble, make your way down to the lower level shops and restaurants. Test your knowledge of mollusks... How many different kinds of oysters do you think there are? Four? Six? Eight? Wrong. At the Grand Central Oyster Bar (the ideal place to meet before the theatre) you may see a dozen different species. Make reservations for eleven of your friends and you'll be able to make a comprehensive taste test. Then, walk outside to see how clever (and controversial) developers placed the Pan Am skyscraper on top of the station. Incidentally, even New Yorkers will advise against the public toilets off the Grand Central Concourse. Use the facilities near the shops and you'll stand a better chance of keeping your oysters down.

UNITED NATIONS

After the second war to end all wars was fought, political leaders thought it would be a good idea to have a place where foreigners could convene to talk out differences instead of shooting at one another. Swiss statesmen, diplomats, chocolatiers and restaurant owners hoped the meeting place would be in Geneva, but John D. Rockefeller, Jr. intervened with an 18-acre site along the East River, which he offered to donate to the cause. Mr. Rockefeller prevailed, and today the United Nations plaza is a contemporary tower of babel. A visit (reservations only) to the delegates dining room will make you instantly aware of our global village. Here, the angriest words spoken are those concerning plantin soup that's too salty, a rooster curry that's cold, or soiled chopsticks. A one-hour guided tour will take you through much of the facility, including a visit to the General Assembly Building with its concentrically curved rows of delegate seating, the well-tended grounds outside the Secretariat Building, and some behind-the-scenes viewing. If the place looks a little too eclectic it's because each nation contributed its own interior design ideas and furnishings.

*Following: Some Toilets
in the Neighborhood*

RCA BUILDING
1250 Ave of the Americas

MEN'S   ★★

NUMBER OF STALLS	6
NUMBER OF URINALS	5
NUMBER OF SINKS	5
CLEANLINESS RATING	FAIR

AMENITIES: Not consistent with the glitzy architecture of Rockefeller Center, this high volume room is lit by fluorescent tubes, sports grungy white tile walls, bad bar soap, and several broken liquid dispensers. The toilet paper is thin, and two out of the three air dryers didn't work.

ACCESSIBILITY: Enter off 6th, go down to the subway concourse, and it's up and right from the lobby.

WHEELCHAIR ACCESS: NO

GENERAL COMMENTS: Hot and muggy; feels like a basement. The more inspiring toilets are not totally public at Rockefeller Center. Implication? You must pay to pee.

WOMEN'S ★★★★

NUMBER OF STALLS   15

NUMBER OF SINKS   7

CLEANLINESS RATING   GOOD

AMENITIES: Rather pedestrian facilities for such an architectural monument, although there are two busy-body attendants on duty, scurrying about under the fluorescent lights. Grey and black tile (a late forties feel), but no lounge. White liquid soap, single-ply white toilet paper, and white paper towels.

ACCESSIBILITY: Clearly marked on the overhead sign on the concourse level; enter off 6th.

WHEELCHAIR ACCESS: NO

GENERAL COMMENTS: Ash trays are visible, but so is a No Smoking sign. Large face mirrors and drinking fountain.

INTERNATIONAL CAFE
630 Fifth Ave.

MEN'S ★★★

NUMBER OF STALLS   2

NUMBER OF URINALS   2

NUMBER OF SINKS   2

CLEANLINESS RATING   GOOD

AMENITIES: Your basic brown and beige; illuminated by one bare light bulb; liquid soap, single-ply tissue, and ample paper towels.

ACCESSIBILITY: Enter from 5th, take the escalator down, circle behind it, then go straight and left into the Cafe.

WHEELCHAIR ACCESS: YES

GENERAL COMMENTS: This cafeteria is one of the cheapest places to eat in the whole neighborhood. Small, bare bones, but adequate. Wheelchair patrons may have trouble with the revolving doors, elevator, and narrow entrance.

WOMEN'S ★★★

NUMBER OF STALLS 3
NUMBER OF SINKS 3
CLEANLINESS RATING FAIR

AMENITIES: It was probably a temporary phenomenon, but there was some trash on the floor, illuminated by one bare light bulb, and surrounded by white and brown tile offset with orange Formica. One big mirror, no connecting lounge, and plenty of pink liquid soap. The paper supply: one-ply white toilet paper, and paper-on-a-roll towels.

ACCESSIBILITY: The sign says Patrons Only, but no one questions you.

WHEELCHAIR ACCESS: YES

GENERAL COMMENTS: Wheelchair patrons may have some trouble with the outside revolving doors and elevator.

McDONALD'S (Time Life Bldg.)
6th Avenue at 50th

MEN'S ★★★★

NUMBER OF STALLS 2
NUMBER OF URINALS 1

NUMBER OF SINKS	2
CLEANLINESS RATING	GOOD

AMENITIES: This franchised toilet is as success-ful as fast food. There's good fluorescent lighting, and the room is pleasantly McTiled and painted, with new plumbing and liquid soap. Very thin one-ply paper, and you air dry hands with a blow-er. The perfumey atmosphere is the result of an over-active automatic deodorizer.

ACCESSIBILITY: Take the stairs from the street, right around the corner from the entrance.

WHEELCHAIR ACCESS: NO
There's a handicapped stall only if you enter from a neighboring building.

GENERAL COMMENTS: The west side of the 6th Avenue concourse level has been re-done to har-monize with the older center. The remodeling is better than the original, and worth seeing.

WOMEN'S ★★

NUMBER OF STALLS	2
NUMBER OF SINKS	2
CLEANLINESS RATING	FAIR

AMENITIES: This McToilet has boxed-in neon light, and displays various kinds of grey tile. The plumbing is quite serviceable, and although there is no lounge, you'll find plenty of liquid soap and one-ply white toilet paper. Air dry.

ACCESSIBILITY: No conspicuous signs, but it is just to the right of the counter in the back.

WHEELCHAIR ACCESS: YES
Revolving and swinging doors, big stalls.

GENERAL COMMENTS: Extra snazzy McDonalds with loads of neon, but a nasty toilet with little ventilation, one sink broken, the other stopped up.

NEW YORK PUBLIC LIBRARY
42nd at Fifth Avenue

MEN'S ★★★

NUMBER OF STALLS	8
NUMBER OF URINALS	3
NUMBER OF SINKS	4
CLEANLINESS RATING	GOOD

AMENITIES: High volume, because we think it's the only one for the entire building. This place conjures up another era, with flickering fluorescent lighting, and vintage marble paneling. The ceiling needs paint, but who looks up? Serviceable plumbing, and hot air machines for drying; thin toilet paper, so be careful.

ACCESSIBILITY: Ask at the information desk, which is always attended. Go through the main entrance, and up the main staircase to the 3rd floor; in the McGraw Rotunda turn left, left, and left again. Behind the partition. Can you see it?

WHEELCHAIR ACCESS: YES
Service elevator at both 42nd St. and 40th St.

GENERAL COMMENTS: Like the rest of the library, this is growing a little shabby with age, but evocative of the grandeur of old New York. You can judge a book by its cover.

WOMEN'S ★★★★

NUMBER OF STALLS	10
NUMBER OF SINKS	4
CLEANLINESS RATING	VERY CLEAN

AMENITIES: For the outdoor lover, there's an open window. You might call this place Faucets in Fresh Air. Fluorescent lighting, institutional marble-and-brass decor, with new metal doors on the stalls. Foam soap, and your choice of air or paper-towel drying.

ACCESSIBILITY: It's on the 3rd floor, south side. The information desk downstairs will guide you.

WHEELCHAIR ACCESS: YES
The door is wide enough, but there are no specific facilities inside.

GENERAL COMMENTS: Flattering, full-length mirrors, and an odd leather-and-stud entry door.

GRAND CENTRAL STATION
42nd between Lexington & Vanderbilt

MEN'S ★

NUMBER OF STALLS	8
NUMBER OF URINALS	8
NUMBER OF SINKS	5
CLEANLINESS RATING	POOR

AMENITIES: Oh-oh! There's a puddle on the floor, the stalls are fouled, and the lighting is all too bright. One might call the decor "hobo chic"; half the plumbing is out of commission, but there's some liquid soap, and you can air-dry your hands if you dare to spend the extra time.

ACCESSIBILITY: Reach it from 42nd off the station's main waiting room; see the homeless shelter to the left.

WHEELCHAIR ACCESS: YES
From 42nd Street

GENERAL COMMENTS: A disgusting facility, notorious citywide. To be shunned; let the homeless vagrants have it.Suggestion: go out onto the platform, find a train that is not due to leave for 10 minutes or so, and use a bathroom on board. It may not be much cleaner, but you can express your disgust in privacy.

WOMEN'S   ★★

NUMBER OF STALLS   20
NUMBER OF SINKS   8
CLEANLINESS RATING   Very Good

AMENITIES: This is a maxi-lav, with plenty of fluorescent lights, a big 5 x 2 foot table, mirrors along one wall (with a handy ledge above the sinks). Smelly pink liquid soap, and four (count 'em) four air dryers. Five of the stalls are called "dressing rooms" (25 cents) but three of those were out of order.

ACCESSIBILITY: Well marked to the right of the main entrance.

WHEELCHAIR ACCESS: YES

GENERAL COMMENTS: A "horoscope scale" is definitely a plus; 98.4% of the women visitors are commuters or tourists. This is not a hostile bathroom.

MEN'S ★★★

NUMBER OF STALLS	4
NUMBER OF URINALS	10
NUMBER OF SINKS	6
CLEANLINESS RATING	GOOD

AMENITIES: No one will accuse the UN of wasting electric power; poor lighting, dark and spotty fluorescent fixtures, and a kind of pale, urine-yellow wall treatment. Good plumbing, though, and liquid soap plungers built into the walls above the row of sinks; three air-dry blowing machines, and plenty of tough toilet paper.

ACCESSIBILITY: Take the elevator to the lower level.

WHEELCHAIR ACCESS: YES

GENERAL COMMENTS: Takes the trophy for the urinal count, but does not reach the same high design standards as the rest of the complex.

WOMEN'S ★★★

NUMBER OF STALLS	14
NUMBER OF SINKS	10
CLEANLINESS RATING	GOOD

AMENITIES: You want space? Try this. Even though the landlords are on an energy conservation kick (poor lighting, very dim surroundings, acid-yellow walls and grey stalls),the plumbing is good and there's a connecting lounge with mirrors and a convenient counter. No chairs, though. Plenty of liquid soap, industrial grade toilet paper, and three working blow dryers.

ACCESSIBILITY: It's on the lower level, well-marked when you get there. You can take the elevator down.

WHEELCHAIR ACCESS: YES

GENERAL COMMENTS: No chance to be claustrophobic. Three big rooms and easy access.

SAKS FIFTH AVENUE
49th & 5th Avenue

MEN'S   ★★★★
NUMBER OF STALLS	6
NUMBER OF URINALS	5
NUMBER OF SINKS	6
CLEANLINESS RATING	GOOD

AMENITIES: Six stalls. No waiting. Move along. Fairly high volume, and a friendly, courteous guard to see that you're not hiding a fur coat under your jacket. Recessed spotlights are bright and pleasant. They show off the nice mahogany, marble, and brass decor. Lots of mirrors, high ceilings, and new plumbing. The soap is liquid and the towels are paper.

ACCESSIBILITY: On the 6th floor, to the left of the elevator bank. Just ask at the information desk on the main level.

WHEELCHAIR ACCESS: YES

GENERAL COMMENTS: Saks obviously just renovated this room. The floor-length mirrors are handy for people who want to check their overall appearance before venturing forth to battle fellow shoppers at the sale racks.

WOMEN'S ★★★

NUMBER OF STALLS	19
NUMBER OF SINKS	6
CLEANLINESS RATING	VERY GOOD

AMENITIES: This is a busy place. Plenty of fluorescent lighting, faded pink tile, and orangey metal stalls. There is a rather dreary connecting lounge with ceiling-to-waist mirrors and a nice ledge for putting packages or purses on. Telephones, six chairs, and a drinking fountain, too. Cardboard-on-a-roll towels.

ACCESSIBILITY: It's inconspicuously located on the 4th floor in the back, which probably deters most visitors.

WHEELCHAIR ACCESS: YES

GENERAL COMMENTS: Smells like oranges, and is surprisingly clean for such a heavily-trafficked room (about ten persons per minute).

If you have good walking shoes and the weather is fine, you might consider an additional landmark on this tour. It's not on our map, but you'll find it easily by either looking almost straight up, or walking due south along Fifth Avenue down to 34th Street...

EMPIRE STATE BUILDING

If you are one of those persons who was plagued by vertigo until you underwent psychotherapy or hypnosis, this is the perfect opportunity to test the efficacy of your cure. Step into the lower concourse of what many regard as the eighth wonder

Lord Kentley W. C. Lemming, shown here with his young son, Flemming,[1] is leading a crusade in England to place small green public toilets up and down the banks of the Thames. Opposed to this movement are two dukes, an earl, and the second cousin of a prince, who contend that a single major lavatory, installed in the Tower of London, would suffice. Lord Lemming was in New York recently to attend a meeting of the Society to Help Improve Toilets, gathering ammunition for a debate that will undoubtedly reach the tiled floor of Parliament. "It's an uphill battle," admits the Lord, "but this could be England's finest hour."[2]

[1] Young Flemming Lemming brought honor to his family by soiling himself on the winding stairway of the Tower of London, demonstrating in this single act the impracticality of placing a public lavatory in this structure. "His brocade jodhpurs were ruined," chortled his father, the Lord, "and we had to throw away his slippers. But we made our point."

[2] The Lord has been known to quote prodigiously from others (without credit) to drive home an argument. In 1977, while campaigning for the replacement of pissoirs in Paris, he recited an entire scene from "Waiting for To Go" in the park along the Champs Elysees. This promptly cleared the boulevard of pedestrians and significantly reduced bench rentals for the day.

of the world (the other seven being considerably shorter) and depicted on the illuminated panels mounted to the lobby walls. Take one of the express, high-speed elevators to the 86th floor, where you'll discover an outdoor promenade, high-altitude food and drink (if your stomach can tolerate it). Also souvenirs of every description, including miniature, injection molded, plastic Empire State Buildings that one can accommodate without a distress bag. If it's open, you may move vertically for another 16 floors to the famed Observatory, where clear weather conditions will enable you to see the panorama of Manhattan, ocean-going vessels 40 miles away, and the neighboring state of New Jersey at a safe distance. Although several newer skyscrapers top the Empire State Building's 1472 feet (built in 1931), none has the honor of a visit by Hollywood bigwig King Kong.

AREA B: CENTRAL PARK PLUS

POINTS OF INTEREST

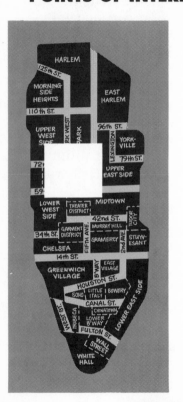

1. **CHILDREN'S ZOO** On a warm day you and your offspring can touch and smell the goats and sheep. Watch where you step.

2. **BIG PERSONS' ZOO** A marvelous place for wandering among the jungle beasts without leaving this continent.

3. **WOLLMAN RINK** In the winter you ought to bring your skates. This is Currier & Ives stuff, up close.

4. **HECKSCHER PUPPET THEATRE** Not always in operation, but a great place to explore, no strings attached.

5. **N.Y. COLISEUM** If you're here during one of the Fancy Food Shows, sneak in for some heavy samples.

6. **LINCOLN CENTER** An architectural musical triumph, especially now that the acoustics have been corrected.

7. **TAVERN ON THE GREEN** Stroll into the park and discover the perfect, ecological dining environment. Let's do lunch.

**8. MUSEUM OF NATU-
RAL HISTORY** Bring a
sandwich. This is
another one of those
enormous facilities that
takes more than 30
minutes to do.

**9. HAYDEN PLANETARI-
UM** Find out all about
the Universe in this
astronomical arena.
Not recommended for
fundamentalists.

Some of the points of
interest are treated in
greater detail on the pages
that follow. Toilet reports,
too. The best time to tour
the Park is daytime. It's
safer then, and you'll see
more. Carry an umbrella if
it looks like rain. You don't
want to spend two hours
under a stone bridge.

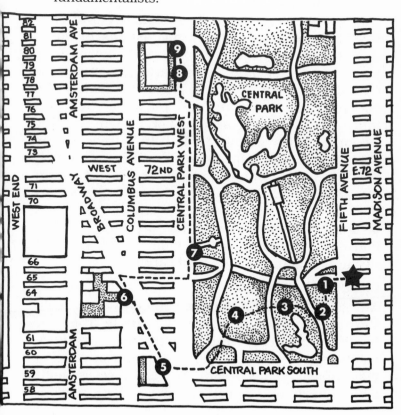

CENTRAL PARK

In the center of Manhattan is an 840-acre micro-cosm of the world's society. In the daytime, French and Swedish nannies push elaborate English baby carriages with their precious American cargoes up and down the pathways, and little children frolic at the petting zoo, while Brazilian joggers and American bikers make their sweaty ways along curving roads that are mostly closed off to automobile traffic. But at night, only brave men in battle gear or policemen dressed as hookers wander into the darkened fields of muggers, robbers and thugs. The fact is, Central Park is New York's last bulwark against the invading developer. Set aside by a few visionaries who knew what was coming, they hired Frederick Law Olmstead and Calvert de Vaux to design the scenic trails and plantings, meadowlands and fountains, skating rink and ponds. On summer evenings (there being strength in numbers) one can observe Shakespearean plays here, or watch the New York Philharmonic or the Metropolitan Opera perform. The best time to see the park is in late afternoon, from the seat of one of the dozens of horse-drawn carriages that ply their way up and down the lanes, compelling joggers to practice hopping and broken field running.

LINCOLN CENTER

Anyone who can hum a tune should visit Lincoln Center, where soul mates in music abound. Dancers, choreographers, instrumentalists, teachers, directors, singers, students and ticket takers have created—with the help of several gifted architects and a plethora of New York millionaires—the city's center of music. Housed in separate buildings are the Metropolitan Opera House, the New York State Theatre, and Avery Fisher Hall. In addition are the Juilliard School of Music, Alice Tully Hall, the Vivian Beaumont and Mitzi E. Newhouse Theatres, the Library and Museum of the Performing Arts, the Guggenheim Bandshell, a spacious plaza, a subway station and a garage, where parking a car can be substantially more expensive than a ticket to the opera. Lincoln Center sounds good now, but as each auditorium was completed it was impugned for its acoustics by performers and music critics alike. More money was raised, and experts armed with thick carpeting, acoustical tile and speaker extension cords found ways to run up construction costs another $8 to $10 million. Clever scheduling gives the Center virtually year-round performances of one kind or another, and although little has been done about the reverberations in the toilets, visitors will find they are never more that a two-or three-minute walk to a clean commode. Waiting in line at intermission may add another 25 more minutes.

THE AMERICAN MUSEUM OF NATURAL HISTORY

Considering that a visit to this four-story building will expose you to (1) birds of the world (2) the 563-carat Star of India star sapphire (3) a slice off a giant sequoia tree (4) and the mummified remains of two hapless dinosaurs, one wonders why this isn't referred to as the American Museum of Unnatural History. Nevertheless, the edifice has particular appeal to those interested in animals, vegetables and minerals, or who squirrel things away in their attics and garages for future reference. The museum (having been reasonably well funded over the years) has had the resources to put most of its accumulated artifacts into cabinets and onto shelves so they may be viewed with envy by other less fortunate packrats. There are frequent lectures, a library containing nearly 400,000 volumes of research information, a cafeteria, and (weather permitting) a sidewalk cafe. There are cultural artifacts that go back thousands of years, and films and slide presentations depicting slimy green plants and crawly things that have already attained stardom on Nova.

Following: Some Toilets
in the Neighborhood

CENTRAL PARK ZOO
Central Park

MEN'S   ★★★

NUMBER OF STALLS	3
NUMBER OF URINALS	3
NUMBER OF SINKS	5
CLEANLINESS RATING	FAIR

AMENITIES: At best, we'd call this place spotty. The hardware is clean but not the floor. The lighting is bright, but the painted cinder blocks are second rate. Nothing special for such a new building. There is liquid soap and air dry machines, but the paper towel dispensers were empty.

ACCESSIBILITY: Clearly marked on the map at

the entrance, but you may have to pay $1.00 admission.

WHEELCHAIR ACCESS: YES

GENERAL COMMENTS: Thankfully large (considering the hordes of kids here) but not well ventilated. One wheelchair stall.

WOMEN'S ★★★

NUMBER OF STALLS 6

NUMBER OF SINKS 5

CLEANLINESS RATING GOOD

AMENITIES: Considering its location, this is an okay facility. Look for a well-lit fluorescent room, beige-painted concrete blocks, liquid soap, but no ladies lounge. There's a drinking fountain, Tampax machine, and a large mirror. The toilet paper was one-ply white, and there are two air dryers, but the paper dispenser was empty.

ACCESSIBILITY: Clearly marked on maps.

WHEELCHAIR ACCESS: YES
Watch out for the turnstile at the entrance.

GENERAL COMMENTS: This place is a bit stuffy, but that condition might diminish on a windy day. It's high traffic, too. You'll have a short wait during peak times.

WOLLMAN RINK
Central Park

MEN'S   ★★★

NUMBER OF STALLS	3
NUMBER OF URINALS	6
NUMBER OF SINKS	3
CLEANLINESS RATING	GOOD

AMENITIES: Be careful. Most of the kids you see on skates are a little unsteady. Overall impression: dim, poorly lit stalls, grimy rubber floor, and a great granite sink counter surrounded by smooth grey tile. New plumbing, liquid soap, single-ply toilet paper and ample paper towels.

ACCESSIBILITY: The cashier may let you in without paying. Ask nicely; it's clearly marked near the entrance.

WHEELCHAIR ACCESS: YES

GENERAL COMMENTS: Spacious, but equipped with a distractingly noisy ventilator; there's one wheelchair stall.

WOMEN'S   ★★

NUMBER OF STALLS	6
NUMBER OF SINKS	3
CLEANLINESS RATING	GOOD

AMENITIES: This is one big uninspired room with fluorescent lights and almost pitch-black walls. You'll find the traditional tiles and plastic laminate, but no soap or towels. Thank heavens there's toilet paper (single-ply white) and several face mirrors to touch up the makeup.

ACCESSIBILITY: Its location is clearly marked, and if you resonate with the cashier on duty you may get to it without paying.

WHEELCHAIR ACCESS: YES

GENERAL COMMENTS: Neither dirty or smelly, but a bit stuffy. The toilets are mounted less than 12 inches off the floor, which is inexplicable, unless the entire facility was designed for pre-pubescent girls.

HECKSHER PUPPET HOUSE
Central Park

MEN'S ★

NUMBER OF STALLS	5
NUMBER OF URINALS	5
NUMBER OF SINKS	1
CLEANLINESS RATING	POOR

AMENITIES: At one time this place was probably nice, but now there is no soap, no towels, but plenty of wet on the floor. In the summer, beware of the flies.

ACCESSIBILITY: Clearly marked on the playground side of the pavilion. You'll find it easily.

WHEELCHAIR ACCESS: YES

GENERAL COMMENTS: Open 8 to 5, but no doors on the stalls.This is one charming building that cries out for rehabilitation and some serious, ongoing maintenance.

WOMEN'S ★

NUMBER OF STALLS	9

NUMBER OF SINKS   1

CLEANLINESS RATING   POOR

AMENITIES: Well, amenities may be a misnomer. It's a bit too dark (with its black metal stalls and brown wall tiles), and there are no towels, no soap, and one-ply white paper.Reminiscent of summer camp.

ACCESSIBILITY: In the Hecksher Puppet Playhouse; marked "Girls".

WHEELCHAIR ACCESS: NO

GENERAL COMMENTS: A most wretched bathroom, with dirt encrusted on the walls. For the desperate only.

CENTRAL PARK (COLUMBUS CIRCLE)
Central Park West At 61st

MEN'S   ★

NUMBER OF STALLS   2

NUMBER OF URINALS   2

NUMBER OF SINKS   2

CLEANLINESS RATING   POOR

AMENITIES: A facility like this is too well lit at any light level. Not nice. Grey tile, dirty terrazzo floors, and 50 percent of the sinks were not working, which left only one operable. But, no soap, no towels, no ambience. The word "stink" comes to mind. Instantly.

ACCESSIBILITY: Not really marked, but you could follow your nose or, in summer, the noise of the flies.

WHEELCHAIR ACCESS: YES

GENERAL COMMENTS: Take this toilet off your visitors list.

CHILDREN'S ZOO
Central Park

MEN'S ★★

NUMBER OF STALLS	2
NUMBER OF URINALS	3
NUMBER OF SINKS	2
CLEANLINESS RATING	FAIR

AMENITIES: Made for children, with super-low sinks and even lower toilets. A bit of filtered natural light, but otherwise dim and dingy, with a decaying fifties look.Needs paint badly. Dripping sinks, and no soap or towels.

ACCESSIBILITY: It's clearly marked on the main floor.

WHEELCHAIR ACCESS: NO

GENERAL COMMENTS: Floor-length urinals. But watch out...the floor is puddled; 10 cent admission.

WOMEN'S ★

NUMBER OF STALLS	4
NUMBER OF SINKS	3
CLEANLINESS RATING	POOR

AMENITIES: The age-old fingerprints on the pink and grey walls are a historic record of another era. Permanent grime combines with the unmistakable aroma of human waste; there's no soap, no paper towels, lots of trash on the floor, and a little bit of single-ply toilet paper left, if you hurry.

ACCESSIBILITY: Easy to see at the right of the entrance.

WHEELCHAIR ACCESS: NO

GENERAL COMMENTS: Pathetic when one considers that this room could be a real image-builder for the Big Apple.

TAVERN-ON-THE-GREEN
Central Park at 63rd

MEN'S   ★★★★

NUMBER OF STALLS	3
NUMBER OF URINALS	2
NUMBER OF SINKS	2
CLEANLINESS RATING	EXCELLENT

AMENITIES: You could spend a quiet hour here. Your countenance will be stage-lit by incandescent spotlights; it's a small and intimate little lounge with multi-hued tobacco-brown tiles and gold faucets. Good toilet paper and abundant paper toweling.

ACCESSIBILITY: On the main floor near the entrance.

WHEELCHAIR ACCESS: YES

GENERAL COMMENTS: Incredibly well stocked; the attendant's radio was tuned to a pleasant jazz station.

WOMEN'S   ★★★★

NUMBER OF STALLS	6
NUMBER OF SINKS	5

CLEANLINESS RATING   EXCELLENT
Almost too clean.

AMENITIES: It's the battle of the air fresheners! Almost too clean, this lavatory has an attentive attendant, it's well lit, and enjoys the companionship of a pleasant connecting lounge. There are three gleaming face mirrors with a handy ledge, lots of liquid soap, white paper towels, and soft, expensive toilet paper.

ACCESSIBILITY: To the right of the entrance. But the management expects you to be a patron (which is a nice experience, too).

WHEELCHAIR ACCESS: NO

GENERAL COMMENTS: This lavatory has all the amenities: hairspray, matches, perfume, etc.

LINCOLN CENTER-METROPOLITAN OPERA
Concourse Level

MEN'S   ★★
NUMBER OF STALLS   2
NUMBER OF URINALS   3
NUMBER OF SINKS   3
CLEANLINESS RATING   FAIR

AMENITIES: Not well staged, this men's room looks dirtier than it actually is. The lighting director selected incandescent spots to illuminate the brown floor and cast an unpleasant reflected glow on the yellow ceiling. Yes, it's old but it's functional. It has liquid soap, single-ply toilet paper, and a full house of paper towels. S.R.O. during intermissions.

ACCESSIBILITY: Near the tour office on the concourse level, and marked on the map in the main plaza.

WHEELCHAIR ACCESS: NO

GENERAL COMMENTS: There may be an occasional vagrant found performing his morning ablutions, but everybody has to go somewhere.

WOMEN'S ★★★★

NUMBER OF STALLS	1
NUMBER OF SINKS	1
CLEANLINESS RATING	Excellent

AMENITIES: A chorus of welcome features, on a diminutive stage. One seat in the house, but the room is large, well- lit, and tiled in white. Liquid soap, paper towels on a roll, and a fine grade of toilet paper.

ACCESSIBILITY: It turns out this is a reserved seat. You'll only be admitted by a guard with a key.

WHEELCHAIR ACCESS: YES

GENERAL COMMENTS: Find the place across from the Metropolitan Opera and Avery Fisher Hall.

LINCOLN CENTER - CONCOURSE LEVEL
Special Handicap Facility

MEN'S ★★★

NUMBER OF STALLS	1
NUMBER OF URINALS	0
NUMBER OF SINKS	1
CLEANLINESS RATING	FAIR

AMENITIES: Bright fluorescent lighting, bounced off small white tiles, with fixtures and plumbing engineered for the handicapped. Liquid soap, paper towels, and good toilet paper.

ACCESSIBILITY: Near the garage beneath the Mitzi Newhouse Theatre. The guard will buzz you in.

WHEELCHAIR ACCESS: YES

GENERAL COMMENTS: A good idea gone awry; this special place could use a good cleaning. It's in grim condition.

WOMEN'S ★★

NUMBER OF STALLS	4
NUMBER OF SINKS	3
CLEANLINESS RATING	PRETTY GRUNGY

AMENITIES: A discordant note, harshly illuminated by fluorescent globes over each stall. Decor: a concerto of beiges, with lots of mirrors, but sadly only one stall flushed, while the others were distinguished only by their broken foot pedals. Yet, there was a large, overheated connecting lounge with four big chairs and floor to ceiling mirrors. For personal hygiene, a duet of liquid soap and paper on a roll.

ACCESSIBILITY: Good. Marked on the outside map in the central concourse.

WHEELCHAIR ACCESS: NO

GENERAL COMMENTS: Interior climate designed for Mephistopheles.

ROY ROGERS/PIZZA HUT RESTAURANT— LINCOLN CENTER
Broadway between 62nd & 63rd

MEN'S ★★

NUMBER OF STALLS	1
NUMBER OF URINALS	2
NUMBER OF SINKS	2
CLEANLINESS RATING	FAIR

AMENITIES: Believe it or not, the stalls are for humans. Fluorescent lighting complements the quarry tile floor and beige tile walls. Lots of non-foaming liquid soap, single-ply paper (with no visible dispenser) and a hot air machine to dry your hands.

ACCESSIBILITY: Find it to the rear of the downstairs seating section.

WHEELCHAIR ACCESS: NO

GENERAL COMMENTS: Good in a pinch because it's on the main drag, but this is obviously a high volume facility.

WOMEN'S ★★

NUMBER OF STALLS	2
NUMBER OF SINKS	2
CLEANLINESS RATING	FAIR

AMENITIES: Trigger may have been through here earlier. Dull paper and paint, in a fluorescent glow that's not too bright. The brick floor is not clean, and although the plumbing sounds impressive, it doesn't work too well. The toilet paper is on the tank (there's no dispenser), and only broken soap and a broken air dryer.

ACCESSIBILITY: Find it downstairs, near the additional seating area.

WHEELCHAIR ACCESS: NO

GENERAL COMMENTS: Everything needs to be fixed. Tell Roy. This is like a frontier toilet.

NEW YORK PUBLIC LIBRARY—LINCOLN CENTER
111 Amsterdam Ave at 64th

MEN'S ★★

NUMBER OF STALLS	2
NUMBER OF URINALS	2
NUMBER OF SINKS	4
CLEANLINESS RATING	FAIR

AMENITIES: You'll discover highly functional plumbing in this fluorescent-lit room, together with stained white tile walls and pale grey floors. Overall there's a vague sixties institutional look. One of the two liquid soap dispensers was working. If this is crowded, there is also a second floor bathroom.

ACCESSIBILITY: In the basement, clearly marked in the lobby of the plaza.

WHEELCHAIR ACCESS: YES

GENERAL COMMENTS: This facility is far from being a family toilet. Aside from the raunchy graffiti, there is clear evidence of non-hygienic activities involving controlled substances.

Dr. Emanual Defecado, an ordained minister of the Episti-chloride Church, is one of those unsung heroes of the toilet wars. He joins with others of the cloth to form an ecumenical advisory council to help sensitize builders, developers and city planners to the growing lavatory needs of the New York visitor. He spends every moment of his free time making unannounced calls on the city's movers and shakers, giving them mimeographed copies of his *List of Ten*, a compelling inventory of changes that must be undertaken to restore the toilet to its former seat of glory. The good doctor is shown here reaching for a pocket pack of sanitary plastic toilet seat covers, to aid a friend inflicted with paranoidal diarrhea.

WOMEN'S ★★★

NUMBER OF STALLS	3
NUMBER OF SINKS	3
CLEANLINESS RATING	GOOD

AMENITIES: No trash or water on the floor, but a pervasive, sickeningly sweet odor. The lights are fluorescent, but it's a bit dark in the stalls. On the walls, beige and white tiles complemented by yellow metal and a scarred Tampax machine; long waist-to-ceiling mirrors with a convenient ledge for makeup. Liquid soap, white quilted paper towels on a roll, and good T.P.

ACCESSIBILITY: Indicated in the elevator.

WHEELCHAIR ACCESS: YES

GENERAL COMMENTS: There is an identically decorated bathroom on the 2nd floor, with twice as many stalls and sinks. Incidentally, the library is a good place to regroup in air-conditioned comfort, and there are public telephones across the hall.

AREA C:
CENTRAL PARK SOUTH

POINTS OF INTEREST

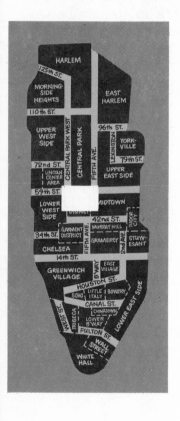

1. CARNEGIE HALL
Famous because of
its proximity to the
Carnegie Deli, where
the steamy corned beef
is imcomparable.

2. ESSEX HOUSE
Famous because of its
proximity to the N.Y.
Athletic Club, where
the drinks and people
are superior.

3. THE PLAZA HOTEL
Where you can still
enjoy Mozart with your
cheesecake in the
Palm Garden. Nice
oyster bar, too.

4. F.A.O. SCHWARZ
No assembly required.
Undeniably a child's
idea of what paradise
must be; 10,000 toys
and games.

5. TRUMP TOWER Pink
marble, shiny brass
and glittering glass,
enclosing the world's
richest retailers.

6. FIFTH AVENUE SHOPPING Gucci, Fortunato, Doubleday, Tiffany and others await you and your gold card.

7. MUSEUM OF MODERN ART The most exciting collection of contemporary art anywhere in the world.

8. AMERICAN CRAFT MUSEUM Proves beyond a doubt that our native craftspeople are good designers, too.

9. N.Y. HILTON The epitome of the N.Y. hotel, with tall doormen, long limos, cocktail lobby, top dining, etc., etc.

On the following pages are a few more details, with appropriate toilet reports on the entire neighborhood. If you have time, wander around the Theatre District (another 6-8 square blocks) or stroll south to Times Square.

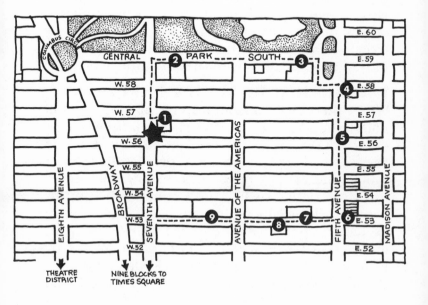

TRUMP TOWER

For those who believe shopping approaches a religious experience, Trump Tower is a cathedral of commerce. Pink, peach and orange marble line its atrium, and branches of the toniest shops in the world are stacked behind glass and brass nearly eight stories high. Above it are another 60 stories of offices and apartments, the uppermost with a price tag of around $10 million. If you're looking for a refrigerator, a monkey wrench, or a box of cornflakes, you'll have to shop elsewhere, at some horizontal mall. Trump Tower is where you go for floor-length ermine robes, perfume in solid gold bottles, or a flawless 14-carat bauble suspended from a heavy platinum chain. If you're an inveterate people watcher, order an expensive cup of coffee in the lower level, lobby restaurant and watch the moving parade of unblinking Arab Sheiks, Drug Kingpins, Oil Magnates and their significant others moving diagonally up and down the soil-free escalators, together with the tourists. The tourists are the ones with their mouths open.

THE MUSEUM OF MODERN ART

When the people upstairs aren't making a lot of noise, the Museum of Modern Art (affectionately called MOMA) is a terrific place to visit. Back in the early eighties, an enterprising developer talked the MOMA board into selling the museum's air rights so he could construct a multistory stack of condominia atop the museum. In exchange, the museum doubled its exhibit space and gets a piece of the condo action. Works by Picasso, Matisse, Jackson Pollack, Jasper Johns, Cezanne, Van Gogh, and many others are found here (even though three-quarters of MOMA's collection must be kept in storage for persisting lack of space). MOMA goes beyond paintings and drawings to include contemporary furniture, the photography of Edward Steichen (who was married to a lady who painted giant flowers), the architectural models of Le Corbusier, classic films, posters, and the famous museum watch. A cafeteria serves modern soup, which can be taken outside to the sculpture garden, except in the winter when the ice-covered chairs dislodge diners. Closed Mondays.

AMERICAN CRAFT MUSEUM

Grownups who can't paint or write good music or poetry, usually resort to crafts. A special museum was built for these people, and a visit here will show you pretty much how their time was spent. Works in clay, fiber, glass, metal, wood, and other more modern materials that are difficult to identify are on exhibit. At one time this museum occupied a brownstone just a block away, but it was small and poorly lit. Ceramic artists and basket weavers who were turned away due to insufficient gallery space complained so much that a fund drive was launched and in 1986 the present structure was opened with four times the room contained in the old location. In the ensuing years, however, more artists joined the ranks of the artsy craftsy, and if rumor is correct, another site will have to be found, or some entrepreneur will purchase air rights to put up another tall apartment building, and devote several floors to additional display space. Until that happens, the existing museum will have to do.

TIMES SQUARE

If sleaze has a home it's on 42nd Street, and where 42nd and Broadway meet, that's Times Square. It may be the world's most famous misnomer, because it is neither a square, nor does the New York Times (for which it was named)) remain there. At one time this was the center of the city, ringed by major motion picture houses, popular clubs and restaurants that catered to Hollywood and Broadway celebrities, and bars that played America's finest jazz. It was a magnet to the kid from Kansas who got off on neon, because signs with letters 50 feet tall blinked and twinkled everywhere. Some things still remain. The signs are still there, but now they promote products from Tokyo, and the movie palaces have become porno houses with sticky floors and single-minded audiences. Most of the clubs have been transformed into hi-fi stores with going-out-of-business signs that bear flyspecks from 1972. One bright spot is a place called TKTS. Every day, unsold seats to New York's finest plays and musicals for that evening go on sale at half-price. The lines for those bargains are often long, but the wait may be worth it. Keep your pockets buttoned here, and refuse to talk to the nice young man who needs subway fare to his mom's house, or the pretty painted lady who has been very lonesome for the last 20 minutes.

Following: Some Toilets
in the Neighborhood

TRUMP TOWER
725 Fifth Ave.

MEN'S   ★★★

NUMBER OF STALLS	4
NUMBER OF URINALS	5
NUMBER OF SINKS	4
CLEANLINESS RATING	GOOD

AMENITIES: The Trump style continues from the atrium into the men's room, with pleasant lighting that flatters your complexion against the peach and orange tile and sunset rouge plastic laminate surfaces. More pleasant than the rest of building, in fact. New plumbing, liquid soap, and lots of soft, absorbent, easily obtained paper towels.

ACCESSIBILITY: Go downstairs. It's hard to find, just near the expensive coffee shop.

WHEELCHAIR ACCESS: YES

GENERAL COMMENTS: Considering the traffic, this place is very well maintained and should be on every tourist's list of places to visit.

WOMEN'S   ★★★

NUMBER OF STALLS	9
NUMBER OF SINKS	5
CLEANLINESS RATING	EXCELLENT

AMENITIES: This is a stadium of a lavatory. Bright fluorescent lighting, and the pink marble of Trump Tower becomes pink tile in the Trump bathroom, with pink Formica stalls. No lounge, though. The liquid soap is an odd shade of green, but the paper towels are white. High-tech, timed release faucets, and both full-length and ceiling-to-sink mirrors.

ACCESSIBILITY: It rests gleaming and majestic on the garden level.

WHEELCHAIR ACCESS: YES
One wheelchair stall.

GENERAL COMMENTS: Come in. The water's fine.

MUSEUM OF MODERN ART
53rd between 5th & 6th

MEN'S   ★★★

NUMBER OF STALLS	2
NUMBER OF URINALS	3
NUMBER OF SINKS	3
CLEANLINESS RATING	FAIR

AMENITIES: Slick, smooth, and modern, with indirect lighting above the mirrors, new plumbing, liquid soap, and contemporary paper goods. But there's a strange, unfamiliar odor that pervades.

ACCESSIBILITY: On the 2nd, 3rd, and 4th floors; also on the main floor, but you'll have to ask. There are also facilities near the museum's restaurant. Come prepared to pay for the privilege.

WHEELCHAIR ACCESS: YES

GENERAL COMMENTS: Modern, sterile, and spacious. Better in many respects than the toilets of the Museum of Modern Art in Paris, should you ever be asked at a cocktail party to make a comparison.

WOMEN'S ★★★

NUMBER OF STALLS	3
NUMBER OF SINKS	3
CLEANLINESS RATING	FAIR

AMENITIES: Fluorescent tubes in steel boxes are mounted over the sinks, illuminating the beige tile, pink liquid soap, and tan paper towels. A tampon machine glimmers on one wall, while three mirrors with a small ledge can be detected along another wall. Handy electrical outlets are discovered here and there, and although there is an odoriferous atmosphere, it's better than the canals of Venice.

ACCESSIBILITY: On the 2nd floor, requiring an admission fee.

WHEELCHAIR ACCESS: YES

GENERAL COMMENTS: A modicum of graffiti adds to the character of this room. In a single word, this W.C. is okay.

AMERICAN CRAFT MUSEUM
40 W. 53rd Street

MEN'S ★★★★

NUMBER OF STALLS	2
NUMBER OF URINALS	2
NUMBER OF SINKS	2
CLEANLINESS RATING	EXCELLENT

AMENITIES: Worth every penny of the price of

admission; a pleasing, brand new facility with well-designed modern sinks. Compact, but not cramped. Clever, framed posters decorate the walls and there is abundant liquid soap, paper towels, and big mirrors.

ACCESSIBILITY: You will need to ask. It's in the basement.

WHEELCHAIR ACCESS: YES

Take the elevator located near the desk; directions are indicated with a small sign.

GENERAL COMMENTS: Nice, clean feeling; must have been designed by a talented American Craft person, thus avoiding the oppressively institutional facilities of most other museums.

WOMEN'S   ★★★★

NUMBER OF STALLS   3
NUMBER OF SINKS   2
CLEANLINESS RATING   VERY CLEAN

AMENITIES: The way toilets ought to be; muted, indirect fluorescent lighting, beige floor tile, and textured, soft-surface walls with no puddles or paper on the floor. Efficient plumbing, a big mirror, and tiny little stools for women in waiting. There's a hook for coats, a ledge for bags, an electrical outlet, liquid soap that really works, and absorbent paper towels.

ACCESSIBILITY: On the lower level, reachable by elevator or stairs. Buy a ticket first.

WHEELCHAIR ACCESS: YES

GENERAL COMMENTS: Reinstates one's faith in the craftmanship of Americans.

PLAZA HOTEL
2 W. 59th (Central Park S)

MEN'S ★★★★

NUMBER OF STALLS 2

NUMBER OF URINALS 3

NUMBER OF SINKS 3

CLEANLINESS RATING EXCELLENT

AMENITIES: Lots of pleasant fellow users, gently illuminated by muted incandescent bulbs and modern stagelights above the polished mirrors. Marble floor, excellent plumbing, good liquid soap and plenty of paper towels for drying; well stocked with colognes, brushes and mouthwash. An attendant on duty.

ACCESSIBILITY: Best to ask. It's on the main floor toward the rear on the 58th St. side. Or, follow the crowd. It's very well attended.

WHEELCHAIR ACCESS: NO
Several steps up from the street.

GENERAL COMMENTS: A toilet befitting such a pre-eminent hotel.

WOMEN'S ★★★★

NUMBER OF STALLS 5

NUMBER OF SINKS 4

CLEANLINESS RATING SUPERIOR

AMENITIES: An attendant on duty to guide you through the grey marble, flowered Victorian wallpaper, and mirrors with Hollywood makeup lights. Excellent plumbing, fine liquid soap, and white, white towels. The toilet tissue is exquisite.

ACCESSIBILITY: There are directional signs if you enter on 5th Ave.

WHEELCHAIR ACCESS: NO

GENERAL COMMENTS: A full Chanel dispensary if you need a midday zap of smell-good.

RUMPELMAYERS/ST. MORITZ
50 Central Park S.

MEN'S ★★

NUMBER OF STALLS	5
NUMBER OF URINALS	4
NUMBER OF SINKS	3
CLEANLINESS RATING	GOOD

AMENITIES: Not up to the level of the elegant restaurant. Fluorescent lighting mounted in an asbestos-tile, dropped ceiling. Ugly but functional. Liquid soap and choice of paper towels or blow dry. (At least the place is deodorized.)

ACCESSIBILITY: No need to enter the restaurant; go through the lobby of the St. Moritz. It's in the back, downstairs.

WHEELCHAIR ACCESS: YES

GENERAL COMMENTS: An eerie sound of subterranean water, coming from behind a crudely padlocked door, lends a mystique to this pastiche of Formica, steel, and vestiges of original art deco.

WOMEN'S ★★★

NUMBER OF STALLS	4
NUMBER OF SINKS	3
CLEANLINESS RATING	GOOD

AMENITIES: A bit worn, but from age, not grime. Fluorescent lighting amid a hodge-podge of remodeling, with its false stucco ceiling, 1930's porcelain tiles, grey marble walls and surprisingly yellow Formica. Pearly white liquid soap, and acceptable toilet tissue.

ACCESSIBILITY: Under the St. Moritz lobby, in back. No need to go through the restaurant (although it's great).

WHEELCHAIR ACCESS: MAYBE
They tried. There's a ramp at the entrance and one large stall, but only a 2 1/2-foot-wide doorway between the lounge and the bathroom.

GENERAL COMMENTS: This toilet has seen better days, but still...in an emergency...

ESSEX HOUSE
160 Central Park South

MEN'S   ★★★★

NUMBER OF STALLS	4
NUMBER OF URINALS	3
NUMBER OF SINKS	3
CLEANLINESS RATING	GOOD

AMENITIES: Another of the world-class hotel facilities, with bright but flattering light, elegant beige marble, and clean tile floors. Spacious and pleasant. Liquid soap by Yardley English Lavender, with real washcloth-size towels, hand lotion, huge floor-length mirrors, and a wall shelf over the sink. A toilet for all seasons.

ACCESSIBILITY: On the main floor, believe it or not, straight ahead from the front door; turn left after the elevators. Inconspicuously marked.

WHEELCHAIR ACCESS: YES

GENERAL COMMENTS: A little wetness around the counter and the urinals, but it could simply be condensation.

WOMEN'S ★★★★

NUMBER OF STALLS 4

NUMBER OF SINKS 4

CLEANLINESS RATING EXCELLENT

AMENITIES: You could bring a client here. Good fluorescent lighting above the stalls and sinks, and Yardley's English Lavender Soap on hand, with 100% cotton hand towels and Kleenex, too. Beige marble and agate stone on the floor and vanity tops, with beige, shell-design wallpaper. Lots of glass, with two walls clad in floor-to-ceiling mirrors.

ACCESSIBILITY: Good. It's marked "Powder Room".

WHEELCHAIR ACCESS: MAYBE
It looks like the second doorway is too narrow.

GENERAL COMMENTS: The two pay phones, stool, ashtray and coat rack are evidence of a thoughtful hotel management.

NEW YORK HILTON
53rd At Ave. of Americas

MEN'S ★★★★

NUMBER OF STALLS 4

NUMBER OF URINALS 9
NUMBER OF SINKS 6
CLEANLINESS RATING EXCELLENT

AMENITIES: Good indirect and direct lighting in a "moderne" seventies decor. Marble floors and vanity tops, excellent plumbing, convenient built-in-plunger liquid soap devices. Excellent paper goods for toilet and hand-drying.

ACCESSIBILITY: Up on the mezzanine, hard to find. It's where all the meeting rooms are.

WHEELCHAIR ACCESS: YES
If you take the elevator instead of the escalator.

GENERAL COMMENTS: A nice place to visit. Lots of space and the entrance is thickly carpeted.

WOMEN'S ★★★★

NUMBER OF STALLS 5
NUMBER OF SINKS 6
CLEANLINESS RATING EXCELLENT

AMENITIES: The twin of the men's room. Good quality liquid soap in handy dispensers, and high-grade toilet paper and paper towels. Everything works.

ACCESSIBILITY: Up on the mezzanine, near the meeting rooms. Designed to accommodate large groups of intense conference and seminar attendees.

WHEELCHAIR ACCESS: YES
Take the elevator instead of the escalator, and punch M for Mezzanine.

GENERAL COMMENTS: A model toilet.

HICKORY HOUSE RESTAURANT
2 E. 45th Street

MEN'S ★★

NUMBER OF STALLS	1
NUMBER OF URINALS	1
NUMBER OF SINKS	1
CLEANLINESS RATING	FAIR

AMENITIES: Step into another era. This is 1939, but the lighting is okay, and so are the plumbing and the liquid soap. But the toilet paper is only fair.

ACCESSIBILITY: Up one steep flight of stairs to the 2nd floor.

WHEELCHAIR ACCESS: NO

GENERAL COMMENTS: There is a nice hand-lettered sign in a frame that cautions everyone to Wash Hands Before Leaving. Crumpled paper towels surrounding the full wastebasket indicate that most visitors take the admonishment seriously.

WOMEN'S ★

NUMBER OF STALLS	2
NUMBER OF SINKS	1
CLEANLINESS RATING	FAIR

AMENITIES: This is tinyness with plumbing. Try not to turn around. Acceptable lighting and liquid soap, with standard quality toilet paper. But why did they mount the paper towel dispenser 6 feet above the floor?

ACCESSIBILITY: Up a steep flight of stairs.

WHEELCHAIR ACCESS: MAYBE

GENERAL COMMENTS: The stalls are small and so is the mirror.

FAO SCHWARZ
Grand Army Plaza 58th at 5th

MEN'S   ★★

NUMBER OF STALLS	2
NUMBER OF URINALS	3
NUMBER OF SINKS	3
CLEANLINESS RATING	FAIR

AMENITIES: A nice place to take the kids. Bright fluorescent lighting, grey and white interior decor. A little institutional, perhaps, but all the sinks are functional with good liquid soap, and your choice of air dry or paper towels.

ACCESSIBILITY: Go ask the talking bear near the escalators. He's on the second-floor mezzanine.

WHEELCHAIR ACCESS: YES

GENERAL COMMENTS: If dad has to maneuver tiny offspring, this is the place for it. The staff is pleasant, and they make a special effort to accommodate parents (or grandparents).

WOMEN'S   ★★★★

NUMBER OF STALLS	4
NUMBER OF SINKS	3
CLEANLINESS RATING	VERY CLEAN

Irena Komodescu and her twin sister Illana were brought to the U.S. by their father, a plastics engineer, in 1937. Her first exposure (so to speak) to American toilet facilities, was an outhouse on a farm just outside Springfield, Ohio, where Mr. Komodescu's second cousin, Zumtok, lived. From that moment, Irena vowed to dedicate her life to the improvement of toilets everywhere. The family later moved to Kohler, Wisconsin, where Dad became wealthy as a designer of toilet seats, and Irena distinguished herself as his assistant in ergonometrics. She and her sister now live in New York, where they both have seats on the board of that city's chapter of the Society to Help Improve Toilets. No one even remembers what Zumtok or Springfield look like.

AMENITIES: You can take the toddlers in here without producing tiny wrinkled noses. You'll revel in the white tile walls and the grey tile floors, with neatly enameled metal stalls. There is a connecting lounge with a full changing table (does Mr. S. know his market?) but, alas, no diapers. Half- and full-size mirrors, one chair, reasonably acceptable liquid soap, and pure white paper towels.

ACCESSIBILITY: It's on the second floor. A talking bear gives directions.

WHEELCHAIR ACCESS: YES

GENERAL COMMENTS: On the door it says "Momma Bear" instead of bathroom. We can forgive that.

AREA D: MUSEUMS AND SHOPPING

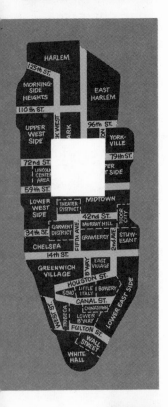

1. THE GUGGENHEIM Frank Lloyd Wright's merry-go-round of a top-heavy museum to house contemporary art.

2. THE METROPOLITAN MUSEUM Maybe you ought to reserve a day or two for this impressive, world-class collection.

3. SAME AS ABOVE, AMERICAN WING Another reason to stay longer. Pick up a free floorplan as you enter.

4. SAN FRANCISCO MODEL MUSEUM Not what you think, fella. This one is full of intricate ship's models.

5. THE WHITNEY MUSEUM Part of New York's cultural triumvirate for contemporary art. A "must" on your tour.

6. RALPH LAUREN Fashion honed to its upscale best; here's what one billion of the world's men and women aspire to.

7. THE LIMITED Jazzy ready-to-wear for women in a glitzy, glamorous environment. Guy stuff, too. Bring your purse and/or wallet.

8. BLOOMINGDALE'S Its aura and image probably exceed its reality, but this department store is still worth a visit.

Most of these points of interest are covered in greater detail on the following pages, together with toilet reports. If you have the time, you might explore a few more of the shops along Lexington Avenue, too, between Bloomingdale's and East 90th Street.

POINTS OF INTEREST

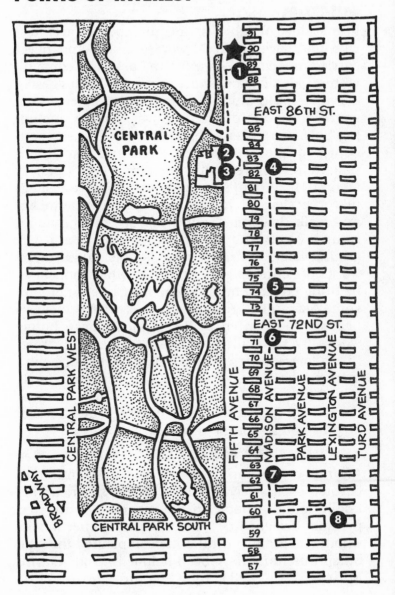

CENTRAL PARK

EAST 86TH ST.

EAST 72ND ST.

CENTRAL PARK SOUTH

CENTRAL PARK WEST

BROADWAY

FIFTH AVENUE

MADISON AVENUE

PARK AVENUE

LEXINGTON AVENUE

TURD AVENUE

THE SOLOMON R. GUGGENHEIM MUSEUM

Frank Lloyd Wright was a contemporary architect who had several wives, wore a cloak, and never carried any cash. When he was asked to come up with an idea for a new art museum, he suggested a round multi-story building, constructed like a spiral. Everyone believed he was serious, including Sol. There was some logic buried in the concept. To avoid the tired back and shoulders usually associated with museum visits ("gallery spine") Mr. Wright's antidote was to have visitors take the elevator to the top of the Guggenheim, and walk downhill around the descending spiral ramp, round and round, until they reach the ground floor. Meantime, one is able to see many works of contemporary art, all of which appear to be hung crooked because the floor tilts. There are some "straight" galleries, too, to help viewers become re-oriented to the planet. These house works by Chagall, Kandinsky, Leger, Cezanne, Pissaro, Renoir, Van Gogh and others who inspired full-length movies. The Guggenheim is closed Mondays. A bookstore, cafe, and outdoor terrace are for persons who become easily nauseated by going around in circles.

THE WHITNEY MUSEUM

After two evictions, New York's only museum devoted exclusively to 20th Century American art finally found a home in the monolithic, inverted pyramid designed by famed Marcel Breuer (about whom one architectural critic complained that the blueprints must have been shipped upside down). Founded in 1931 by Gertrude Vanderbilt

Whitney, a wealthy lady who fancied herself a sculptress, and who was urged to pursue her work by self-serving chauffeurs, butlers, doormen, and two or three cooks. She chose a building on 8th Street as the Museum's original site. It's now occupied by an alternative school. In 1954 the Whitney moved to a place behind the Museum of Modern Art, which promptly acquired it. Today, visitors can cross a concrete entry bridge overlooking a marvelous sculpture garden. Within its galleries are works by Stuart Davis, Jasper Johns, Adolph Gottlieb, Jim Dine and others. There are three branches of the Whitney Museum, one each in the Phillip Morris building, The Equitable Center, and at the Federal Reserve Plaza, so no one has the excuse that it was just too far out of the way. The main museum is closed Mondays.

METROPOLITAN MUSEUM OF ART

Occupying a portion of Central Park, with its main entrance on Fifth Ave., the Metropolitan Museum of Art attracts thousands of visitors every month interested in seeing old stuff. It is an enormous building, with many different wings named after wealthy folks who donated the construction costs and/or the funds to purchase their contents: The ancient Egyptian Temple of Dendur is reassembled brick by brick in one wing, Musical instruments of the past occupy another, plus art from Islam and the Near East. Costumes, Ancient Chinese, Roman and Greek art, and the works of many other dead persons are on display in other galleries. It would take a month to do the Metropolitan Museum justice, and that includes more than a week of being lost in its labyrinth of rooms. In 1987, the Lila Acheson Wallace Wing was added to compete with the Museum of Modern Art, up the street. The Wallace addition contains ten galleries devoted to lesser known 20th-Century artists. Arguably the most fascinating exhibit is the Metropolitan's museum store where reproductions can be purchased at a fraction of the cost of the originals. Closed Mondays.

Following: Some Toilets
in the Neighborhood

METROPOLITAN MUSEUM OF ART
5th Ave. at 82nd

MEN'S ★★

NUMBER OF STALLS	3
NUMBER OF URINALS	2
NUMBER OF SINKS	2
CLEANLINESS RATING	FAIR

AMENITIES: Grim and dim, but surprisingly comfortable considering the volume of use. Grey tile, unimpressive plumbing, undistinguished liquid soap, and paper towels.

ACCESSIBILITY: In the basement, left of the lobby.Don't try to find this facility without a map or a guide. You'll have to pay to use.

WHEELCHAIR ACCESS: YES
Use the somewhat circuitous elevator route, and watch out for the steps at the entrance.

GENERAL COMMENTS: Busy, but there's an antechamber with mirror and drinking fountain.

WOMEN'S ★★

NUMBER OF STALLS	3
NUMBER OF SINKS	2
CLEANLINESS RATING	FAIR

AMENITIES: The odor of an attic prevails, with papers and trash on the floor. It's so dark in the stalls you can barely see your knees. What was once light blue is now pale grey, on the tiles, floors and walls. There's a mirror with a Formica ledge five feet long, and the plumbing works. Useless liquid foam soap, brown stiff paper towels on a roll. In the anteway is one chair and a water fountain. A vending machine for sanitary napkins is the only bright note in the decor.

ACCESSIBILITY: It's marked on the floorplan, but you'll have trouble finding it. Also, you'll have to pay to pee.

WHEELCHAIR ACCESS: YES
There's a special wheelchair toilet on the ground floor.

GENERAL COMMENTS: Not as well maintained as the rest of the structure. Shabby but utilitarian.

METROPOLITAN MUSEUM OF ART
(American Wing) Back 1st floor

MEN'S ★★★

NUMBER OF STALLS	2
NUMBER OF URINALS	3
NUMBER OF SINKS	2
CLEANLINESS RATING	GOOD

AMENITIES: Much newer than the rest of the museum. This facility sports pleasant, muted lighting, rich marble walls and a clean floor. Good mirrors, excellent plumbing, and serviceable liquid soap and paper towels. A little drippy because the towel dispensers are inexplicably located across the room from the sink.

ACCESSIBILITY: Use the map, which you'll find much more practical than the signage.

WHEELCHAIR ACCESS: YES

GENERAL COMMENTS: This toilet is more convenient to the permanent gallery spaces. More spacious, and less frenetic than the old one in the basement near the entrance. Must pay to use

WOMEN'S ★★★★

NUMBER OF STALLS   4

NUMBER OF SINKS   3

CLEANLINESS RATING   EXCELLENT

AMENITIES: Recessed lighting, green marble floors, sturdy metal stalls, beige marble walls and well ventilated. The top two feet along the walls are attractively mirrored, and there's plenty of liquid soap, but the white paper on a roll was all but used up. Nice big mirror with a makeup ledge, and a Tampax machine, too.

ACCESSIBILITY: You'll need a map to find this one, and if you're a vagrant without funds it will be impossible to use.

WHEELCHAIR ACCESS: YES
There's a special handicapped stall.

GENERAL COMMENTS: A very pleasant place.

WHITNEY MUSEUM
Madison Ave at 75th

MEN'S ★★★

NUMBER OF STALLS	1
NUMBER OF URINALS	2
NUMBER OF SINKS	2
CLEANLINESS RATING	GOOD

AMENITIES: Nothing here is superior. The lighting is bright but not flattering. The flooring is pleasant (quarry tile), but undistinguished. And the plumbing is functional but unremarkable. Bar soap, paper towels, and blow-dry machines.

ACCESSIBILITY: In the basement, with swift elevator access. Buy a ticket first, unless you have a student I.D.

WHEELCHAIR ACCESS: YES

GENERAL COMMENTS: Armchair architects would suggest, in retrospect, that another 100 square feet would be an asset to this facility, and save scraped elbows and worn trouser knees.

WOMEN'S ★★★

NUMBER OF STALLS	4
NUMBER OF SINKS	2
CLEANLINESS RATING	GOOD

AMENITIES: Better in many respects than the men's counterpart. Try to disregard the paper on the floor (there was none on the rolls). Good lighting, quarry tile floor, white walls, Tampax machine, and functional plumbing. Messy bar soap, and your option of air dry or paper towels. There is a connecting lounge with one couch and one chair, two prints, a rug, and a lit mirror with ledge, plus a full-length mirror on the side. This is a pay-to-use, pay-to-shmooze kind of place.

ACCESSIBILITY:

WHEELCHAIR ACCESS: YES
There's a handicap stall and sink, too.

GENERAL COMMENTS: Odor free, reasonably clean, and a nice retreat. Maybe the framed prints are rotated every week, which would be an artistic accomplishment.

GUGGENHEIM MUSEUM
5th Ave. between 88th & 89th

MEN'S   ★★

NUMBER OF STALLS	1
NUMBER OF URINALS	0
NUMBER OF SINKS	1
CLEANLINESS RATING	FAIR

AMENITIES: This is not an exalted monument to bodily function; one of two bulbs needed replacing, and the unpainterly off-white walls are not artistic, although even the most meticulous critic would have to admit the plumbing, liquid soap, and paper towels are acceptable. This is a small room—tiny, even—but it owes much of its discomfort to an indifferent architect and unanticipated over-use.

ACCESSIBILITY: On the main floor near the elevators.

WHEELCHAIR ACCESS: YES

It will be a tight fit for a wheelchair to slip through the door.

GENERAL COMMENTS: An afterthought of a toilet in an uncommon building.

WOMEN'S   ★★★

NUMBER OF STALLS	1
NUMBER OF SINKS	1
CLEANLINESS RATING	GOOD

AMENITIES: Remarkably small, with paper all over the floor,and only two bulbs (which are enough because of the room's dimensions). Beige paint, mixed-media terrazzo floor, thick green liquid soap, and stiff white towels on a roll. There is one facial mirror with a spotted glass ledge, a Tampax machine, and those distressing, timed faucets that won't stay on.

ACCESSIBILITY: This is on the ground floor, and there are others on each floor, but you'll have to come up with an admission fee.

WHEELCHAIR ACCESS: NO

GENERAL COMMENTS: The paintings are far more attractive.

BLOOMINGDALE'S
59th & Lexington

MEN'S   ★★

NUMBER OF STALLS	4
NUMBER OF URINALS	3
NUMBER OF SINKS	3
CLEANLINESS RATING	GOOD

AMENITIES: Well, the lighting is not great, and the tile is from the fifties (flesh with beige accents), but everything is functional. Liquid soap, paper towels, good toilet paper. Somebody ought to clean the sinks occasionally.

ACCESSIBILITY: Tough. On the 5th & 7th floors toward the north side of the building. Take an elevator, head east, and find it in a back corridor. It's listed at the main entrance directory and in the elevators.

WHEELCHAIR ACCESS: NO

GENERAL COMMENTS: Needs more ventilation in the summer.

WOMEN'S ★★★★

NUMBER OF STALLS	30
NUMBER OF SINKS	16
CLEANLINESS RATING	VERY CLEAN

AMENITIES: No odor, not even a wisp of deodorant.Cleaning ladies keep everything sparkling, and the fluorescent lighting is placed so you can see in the stall.Black metal dividers and beige ceramic sinks (kind of Chanel-like). Long mirrors, with good liquid soap, and quite acceptable paper towels and toilet tissue.

ACCESSIBILITY: Listed on the store directory and on a nearby wall.

WHEELCHAIR ACCESS: YES

GENERAL COMMENTS: Unusual, and there's an electrical outlet in the stalls (so you can shave?). No lounge, but pleasant nonetheless.

THE LIMITED
62nd & Madison Ave.

MEN'S (UNISEX)   ★★★★

NUMBER OF STALLS	1
NUMBER OF URINALS	1
NUMBER OF SINKS	1
CLEANLINESS RATING	Good

AMENITIES: A remarkable example of good reno-
vation; pink textured wallcovering and pink
Travertine marble. New plumbing, with grab bars
for the handicapped. Excellent soap and paper
products, but a little drippy around the sink.

ACCESSIBILITY: Ask any friendly salesperson.
It's in back, on the main floor.

WHEELCHAIR ACCESS: YES
Watch out for the narrow hall near the main
entrance.

GENERAL COMMENTS: Pleasant, private, and
most of all—pink!

RALPH LAUREN
72nd & Madison Ave.

MEN'S   ★★★★

NUMBER OF STALLS	1
NUMBER OF URINALS	3
NUMBER OF SINKS	3
CLEANLINESS RATING	EXCELLENT

AMENITIES: Very impressive style. Would you
expect anything less from Ralph? Perfect vintage
lighting, spectacularly decorated, with framed art

Illana Komodescu arrived in New York with her twin sister, Irena (see page 94) in 1977. Since then her life has been one mad scramble to locate and identify the worst toilets in Manhattan. At first, she labored on her own, taking notes and writing letters. Later, as a director of the Society to Help Improve Toilets, she led a group of fellow members in a sit-in at the Guggenheim lavatory to bring media attention to the cramped design of that facility. They were ignored by the press until, 21 days later, they were hauled, bent, tired and hungry, to the Society's headquarters, where each was presented with a silver chamber pot, that organization's highest award for courage and persistence. It wasn't until years later that Irena (the twin) admitted that they would have busted out after an hour or two but the door was jammed.

and piped-in jazz. The plumbing is Neo-Victorian with brass fittings. The soap is liquid and the towels are paper.

ACCESSIBILITY: In the basement, not well marked, and also up on the 4th floor.

WHEELCHAIR ACCESS: YES

GENERAL COMMENTS: The atmosphere is pleasantly nostalgic, and newspaper pages are thoughtfully reproduced above the urinals so you'll keep your eyes up front, perhaps.

WOMEN'S   ★★★★
NUMBER OF STALLS   3
NUMBER OF SINKS   3
CLEANLINESS RATING   IMPECCABLE

AMENITIES: Real bulbs in nice lamps. White tile (like a Park Avenue 1930's duplex) in beige and brass. The toilets flush quietly, like the one in your own home. No connecting lounge, but that's because the whole bathroom is a lounge; a porcelain table with face mirror, and paper towels like soft white dinner napkins. The liquid soap could be better.

WHEELCHAIR ACCESS: YES

GENERAL COMMENTS: Worth visiting, just to hear Louis Armstrong over the sound system.

AREA E: GREENWICH VILLAGE

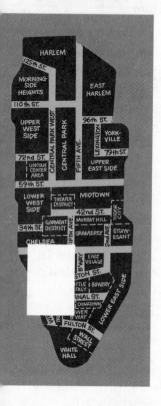

1. GREENWICH VILLAGE Begin your tour by slowly walking south along Fifth Ave. from 14th St. and soon you'll arrive at...

2. WASHINGTON SQUARE Playgrounds, a pool, a big stone arch, street musicians, children and joggers. Very New York.

3. GREENWICH AVENUE You can walk faster now. This is people-watching at its best. Lots of bars and restaurants, too.

4. DEAN AND DELUCA'S The city's most brilliant, tantalizing collection of prepared (and unprepared) foods.

5. FOOD That's its name. For decades, a sunny, comfortable, dining cooperative for the locals. Now open to you transients, too.

6. ENCHANTED FOREST SHOP Like your Aunt Emma's attic, only lots better. Bring young children to help you ferret.

7. CASTELLI'S GALLERY Famous artists, and artists on the verge of fame. One of many galleries in the neighborhood.

8. THINK BIG Aspirin tablets as big as a tire; toothbrushes 4 ft. long; pencils 6 ft. tall. You get the idea.

On the pages that follow you'll find detailed information to help you locate acceptable facilities. This area hardly needs a map. Any block you walk or corner you turn opens a whole new vista of sights and smells. You'll have fun here.

POINTS OF INTEREST

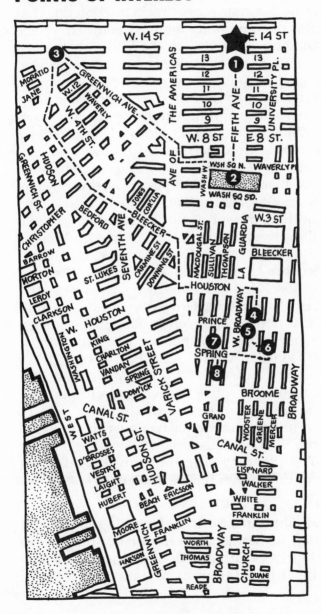

GREENWICH VILLAGE

If it is true, as many New Yorkers contend, that the center of community life in Greenwich Village is Washington Square, then the Village is in deep trouble. That is because day or night it is peopled with a fearful combination of amateur bluegrass musicians, scruffy guitarists singing to themselves, persons who appear to be in alien costumes (their actual street clothes), and elderly skateboarders. Considering that this was an execution site in the late 1700's and later became the burial place for 10,000 plague victims, it may take yet another century for things to get cleaned up. Meantime, move beyond the square and you'll get a glimpse of the artistic side of the Village, where Eugene O'Neill, Frank Norris, O. Henry, and Theodore Dreiser lived and worked. Here too are the so-called off-Broadway theatres, the buildings of New York University, and the well-tended row houses of the city's elite professionals. The air here was breathed by e.e. cummings, Edna St. Vincent Millay, John Barrymore, Dylan Thomas, Bret Harte, and John Masefield. The interesting shops, coffee houses, restaurants, and galleries are so numerous it would be best to reserve a full day or two for meandering. If you're there on a Sunday, forget about using the toilet in the N.Y.U. Library (the only public building unlocked) unless you have a student I.D. card.

SOHO

Lower Manhattan's SoHo has nothing to do with its London namesake. It is an area of roughly 30 square blocks SOuth of HOuston Street, that was once the inhabitance of artists and writers searching for cheap loft space and easy access to the carry-out foods at Dean & DeLuca's. That was about 15 years ago. Then, as rents began to rise, so did the caliber of residents. Stock brokers, investment bankers, department store heiresses, nail artists, rock stars, fashion designers, psychoanalysts and real estate developers moved in. They took another look at the old cast iron factories and warehouses, had them deveined and retrofitted with new pipes and wiring, and thus created another fashionable old neighborhood. The displaced painters and writers moved further south, but a glance at any map will reveal their frightening fate; in a decade they'll be pushed into the viscous confluence of the Hudson and East Rivers, where, because of their body orifices, certain death lurks. Yet a stroll among their former SoHo homes will be a tour through one of the most fascinating agglomerations of trendy stores, shops, excellent restaurants, clever bars, theatres, cafes and galleries seen anywhere in the world. And nearly every cafe has at least one unisex commode. It is a walker's paradise.

Following: Some Toilets in the Neighborhood

MANHATTAN BISTRO
129 Spring Street

MEN'S ★★

NUMBER OF STALLS	1
NUMBER OF URINALS	1
NUMBER OF SINKS	1
CLEANLINESS RATING	GOOD

AMENITIES: The typical bistro W.C., dimly lit, nice interior, acceptable decor, and semi-acceptable toilet paper. Practical and utilitarian.

ACCESSIBILITY: Down a long flight of stairs.

WHEELCHAIR ACCESS: NO

GENERAL COMMENTS: Pleasant, but no soap, no towels, and (fortunately) no purchase necessary.

WOMEN'S   ★★★

NUMBER OF STALLS	2
NUMBER OF SINKS	1
CLEANLINESS RATING	GOOD

AMENITIES: Better by actual comparison to its male counterpart: big mirrors, pleasantly decorated walls, and quite clean, with a comfortable connecting lounge. The liquid soap dispenser needed soap, but the toilet paper was in good supply.

ACCESSIBILITY: Downstairs, with signs telling how to get there.

WHEELCHAIR ACCESS: NO

GENERAL COMMENTS: Spacious, nice decor, a reasonable destination for your convenience stop.

SPRING STREET BAR & RESTAURANT
162 Spring Street

MEN'S   ★★★

NUMBER OF STALLS	1
NUMBER OF URINALS	1
NUMBER OF SINKS	1
CLEANLINESS RATING	GOOD

AMENITIES: You'll like this toilet. It's old fashioned, but with little touches of high-tech. An interesting room with more than adequate plumbing, a good supply of liquid soap and paper towels, and lots of quality toilet paper.

ACCESSIBILITY: It's easy to find, on the main floor.

WHEELCHAIR ACCESS: YES

GENERAL COMMENTS: The establishment itself has a pleasant staff, and no purchase necessary to use the facilities.

WOMEN'S ★★★

NUMBER OF STALLS	1
NUMBER OF SINKS	1
CLEANLINESS RATING	GOOD

AMENITIES: Welcome to a thoughtful, modern toilet, with good lighting and a fine connecting lounge. Small but neat and clean. There are big mirrors, and ample supplies of liquid soap, toilet paper, and thirsty paper towels.

ACCESSIBILITY: Right in front of you as you walk in.

WHEELCHAIR ACCESS: YES

GENERAL COMMENTS: It's unnecessary to be a patron to use this room, but you'll want to. Big, clean mirrors, and just enough space to restore your makeup.

CINCO DE MAYO
349 W. Broadway

MEN'S ★★★★

NUMBER OF STALLS	1
NUMBER OF URINALS	0
NUMBER OF SINKS	1
CLEANLINESS RATING	EXCELLENT

AMENITIES: For those who are not claustrophobic and appreciate a little privacy, this room is well lit, thoughtfully decorated, and boasts new plumbing, liquid soap, and a machine to blow-dry your wet hands.

ACCESSIBILITY: On the main floor, in the back of the restaurant.

WHEELCHAIR ACCESS: NO

GENERAL COMMENTS: A comfortable room for one.

WOMEN'S ★★★

NUMBER OF STALLS	1
NUMBER OF SINKS	1
CLEANLINESS RATING	GOOD

AMENITIES: Larger than the men's room, with similarly good lighting and modern decor. There are clean mirrors on three walls, and ample liquid soap, toilet paper, and the option of paper towels or blow drying.

ACCESSIBILITY: On the main floor, with no signs, but easy to find.

WHEELCHAIR ACCESS: NO

GENERAL COMMENTS: Spacious, clean, and new.

BORGIA II CAFE
161 Prince Street-SoHo

MEN'S ★★

NUMBER OF STALLS 1

NUMBER OF URINALS 0

NUMBER OF SINKS 1

CLEANLINESS RATING GOOD

AMENITIES: Bring a flashlight. No decor, old-fashioned plumbing, but it works. There's bar soap, conventional toilet paper, and plenty of paper towels. It's an okay kind of toilet.

ACCESSIBILITY: The cafe itself is so small, you can't miss the toilet.

WHEELCHAIR ACCESS: YES

GENERAL COMMENTS: The management is much more hospitable if you're a cafe customer; purchase is obligatory.

WOMEN'S ★★

NUMBER OF STALLS 1

NUMBER OF SINKS 1

CLEANLINESS RATING GOOD

AMENITIES: A candle would help. Only fair marks for the lighting, and (simply stated) old interior, old plumbing, old mirror, and old bar soap. The toilet paper is new and so are the paper towels.

Alfred Ofal is a toilet investigator. It is because of his efforts, and those of his colleagues, that a guidebook like this could be conceived and executed. He is officious, fair, diligent and energetic, and, as he freely admits to anyone who will listen, "...I love my work. Perhaps it was my pre-med education that makes me feel so well qualified for the job." There were, of course, a few complaints from visitors who objected to someone standing behind them with a clipboard and pen, but Mr. Ofal's true value reached its nadir when—in an emergency— he would don a woman's disguise to fill in for an occasionally indisposed female colleague. One such person was Shirley Pasternak, a successful uptown painter and toilet inspector, who readily admits "...Ofal often saved the day for me."

ACCESSIBILITY: Right near the front door on the main floor.

WHEELCHAIR ACCESS: YES

GENERAL COMMENTS: Small, old, but absolutely adequate.

AREA F:
LITTLE ITALY & CHINATOWN

1. A GOOD PLACE TO START
Little Italy is packed with some of New York's finest restaurants...often little family-run operations with mama in the kitchen and her kids on the floor, with pop making wine in the basement. Several excellent Italian grocery stores, too, if you want to take home some fresh, imported antipasto, odd-shaped noodles, or irresistible cookies. The bakeries ain't bad, neither.

2. ANOTHER GOOD PLACE TO START Chinatown, like its neighboring area to the north, is a gustatory delight. Restaurants, food shops, and import shops (for low-priced silks and woven baskets, apparel and place settings) can keep you and your spouse occupied for hours.

It's counter-productive to do a dotted-line walking map. Instead, we suggest you move aimlessly about each neighborhood, and stop anywhere for food (Italian or Asian). It will be good.

POINTS OF INTEREST

LITTLE ITALY

Just east of SoHo lies an ethnic area that remains largely unchanged (though considerably smaller) since its birth around the turn of the century. Little Italy spawned some of America's greatest musical and artistic talents, and some of the most successful criminal minds in the world. Efforts to help preserve the community by taking over the old precinct station and remodeling it into an Italian Center failed for lack of funds. And although third and fourth generation Italian Americans have followed others to the suburbs, there are still enough family-owned Italian restaurants and food stores to make exploration of Little Italy (especially at mealtime) a rewarding excursion. Forty varieties of pasta, spicy sausage and pepper sandwiches, calzone, steamy pavarotti rolls, zeppole, and hot veal and chicken prepared Sicilian style should keep you on your gastronomic toes. If you're in New York during early September, Little Italy's entrepreneurs block off the streets and move their businesses outside to handle the hungry crowds, all in honor of San Gennaro, the patron saint of marinara.

CHINATOWN

There is a fascinating but not always successful effort to transform about 12 city blocks of lower Manhattan into a little piece of Peking (or Beijing, as the People's current rulers would have it called). Pagodas on top of the tenements that line the narrow streets help. And so do the colorful banners on storefronts and apartment facades. Even the sidewalk telephone booths resemble glass-walled temples. If you're addicted to old detective stories you might expect an occasional Asian to stagger out of a restaurant with a cleaver in his clavicle, but the tong wars in Chinatown subsided weeks ago. What reigns supreme now is Chinese cuisine. Perhaps the best in the western hemisphere. And the variety will enable you to spend a week here without repeating a meal (no pun intended). The locals are reserved and dignified, and speak their own dialects among themselves. But when the Chinese New Year comes around, these folks turn it into an Asian Mardi Gras with giant dragons and fireworks. An enlightening Chinese museum at the gateway to the area is worth a visit. You'll see artifacts, block prints, deities and coins that long predate Roman civilization. A short walk west of Chinatown and you're in an emerging, trendy area called Tribeca (Triangle Below Canal) which underscores the New Yorkers' affinity for acronyms. What will happen when they link Sullivan, Hudson, Ingram and Thomas? Only time will tell.

*Following: Some Toilets
in the Neighborhood*

CAFE NAPOLI
191 Hester Street

MEN'S ★★

NUMBER OF STALLS	1
NUMBER OF URINALS	0
NUMBER OF SINKS	1
CLEANLINESS RATING	GOOD

AMENITIES: Good lighting, but, momma mia, the sink drips terribly. You'll have to jiggle the toilet (a common plumbing malady). No soap, only ordinary toilet paper, and paper towels of no particular distinction.

ACCESSIBILITY: Kind of hidden behind the bar

WHEELCHAIR ACCESS: YES

GENERAL COMMENTS: Minuscule, barely room for one person, yet for some inexplicable reason, crowded with toilet cleaning supplies.

WOMEN'S   ★★

NUMBER OF STALLS   1

NUMBER OF SINKS   1

CLEANLINESS RATING   FAIR

AMENITIES: Good lighting, but only one small mirror.Bar soap, not uncommon toilet paper, and, for your hands: paper towels.

ACCESSIBILITY: Hidden behind the counter and hard to find.

WHEELCHAIR ACCESS: NO

GENERAL COMMENTS: Needs a good cleaning. Very small, not very comfortable, but hey, any port in a storm, right?

MARE CHIARO
176 ½ Mulberry Street

MEN'S   ★★

NUMBER OF STALLS   1

NUMBER OF URINALS   2

NUMBER OF SINKS   1

CLEANLINESS RATING   FAIR

AMENITIES: It's hard to know where to start. Dim lighting, a dark old interior, but the plumbing works. No soap or towels, and the toilet paper can only be characterized as average.

ACCESSIBILITY: Check behind the bar and there it is.

WHEELCHAIR ACCESS: NO

GENERAL COMMENTS: Look at the ceiling. Missing tiles and plaster gives this room a sort of old world charm.

WOMEN'S

★

NUMBER OF STALLS	1
NUMBER OF SINKS	1
CLEANLINESS RATING	POOR

AMENITIES: You'll be pleased with the lighting, but the decor is old; broken mirrors, no soap, and no towels. Cheer up. There's average toilet paper.

ACCESSIBILITY: Back of the coffee shop.

WHEELCHAIR ACCESS: YES

GENERAL COMMENTS: Not pleasant, quite old, and we'll wager it's not nearly as clean as your bathroom at home.

FERRARA'S
195 Grant Street

MEN'S

★★★

NUMBER OF STALLS	3
NUMBER OF URINALS	3
NUMBER OF SINKS	2
CLEANLINESS RATING	GOOD

AMENITIES: We can report good lighting, abundant (fragrant) liquid soap, and (bless the management), soft toilet paper and plenty of paper towels.

ACCESSIBILITY: Here's the rub. It's hard to find. Make your way to the back of the cafe and then go up one flight of stairs.

WHEELCHAIR ACCESS: NO

GENERAL COMMENTS: An attempt to please. It's large, though a little deficient in decor, and it has no graffiti. Entrance is through a large wooden door.

WOMEN'S ★★★★

NUMBER OF STALLS 3

NUMBER OF SINKS 2

CLEANLINESS RATING EXCELLENT

AMENITIES: The ladies' does it better than the men's. This toilet is very nicely decorated, with big mirrors and a comfortable lounge. Liquid soap, nice toilet paper, and you choose between electric blow-dry or paper towels.

ACCESSIBILITY: Follow the signs. It's upstairs near the men's room.

WHEELCHAIR ACCESS: NO

GENERAL COMMENTS: Clean and pleasant, spacious and fresh-smelling. This is as good as it gets. Bring a camera. You may want pictures.

ROAD TO MANDALAY
380 Broome Street

WOMEN'S   ★★★★

NUMBER OF STALLS   1
NUMBER OF SINKS   1
CLEANLINESS RATING   EXCELLENT

AMENITIES: Good lighting, and would you believe flowers? Lots of mirrors (polished clean), with liquid soap and plenty of paper towels.

ACCESSIBILITY: Search for it at the back of the restaurant.

WHEELCHAIR ACCESS: YES

GENERAL COMMENTS: Pleasant, well-decorated. A nice place to stop for a while. But with only one stall, don't tarry.

20 MOTT STREET RESTAURANT
20 Mott Street, curiously enough

MEN'S   ★★★★

NUMBER OF STALLS   1
NUMBER OF URINALS   2
NUMBER OF SINKS   1
CLEANLINESS RATING   EXCELLENT

AMENITIES: It's hard to know where to begin; superb lighting, spotless marble decor, fine-smelling liquid soap, user-friendly, super soft toilet paper, and sanitary paper towels.

ACCESSIBILITY: You'll have to ask directions; it's down one flight of stairs.

WHEELCHAIR ACCESS: NO

GENERAL COMMENTS: Spacious, plenty of room to move around, stylish, with ash trays on the urinals.

WOMEN'S ★★★★

NUMBER OF STALLS 2
NUMBER OF SINKS 2
CLEANLINESS RATING EXCELLENT

AMENITIES: Compares favorably with its male counterpart; excellent lighting, two big mirrors, fine-smelling liquid soap, good quality toilet paper, but this facility opts for air-drying instead of paper towels.

ACCESSIBILITY: You'll find it downstairs, but there's no sign to direct you.

WHEELCHAIR ACCESS: NO

GENERAL COMMENTS: Welcome home. This lavatory is spacious and pleasant, well-decorated, clean and comfortable. Enjoy.

GOLD & SILVER RESTAURANT
73 Mott Street

MEN'S ★★

NUMBER OF STALLS 1
NUMBER OF URINALS 0
NUMBER OF SINKS 1
CLEANLINESS RATING FAIR

AMENITIES: Dim lighting greets you as you enter. Decor? No decor. Cold water in the faucets, but the plumbing works. Bar soap, paper towels, and the toilet paper is adjudged as okay.

ACCESSIBILITY: You'll have to buy your way in. It's in the back of the restaurant.

WHEELCHAIR ACCESS: YES

GENERAL COMMENTS: Dirty soap, and the place is not very clean.

WOMEN'S   ★★

NUMBER OF STALLS   1

NUMBER OF SINKS   1

CLEANLINESS RATING   FAIR

AMENITIES: Here there is one small mirror, and absolutely no lounge or special decor. Bar soap, ordinary toilet paper, and conventional paper towels.

ACCESSIBILITY: There's a sign, but it's at the back of restaurant. The management would like it better if you were a patron.

WHEELCHAIR ACCESS: NO

GENERAL COMMENTS: Tiny, old, and the door doesn't close well.

SUN TONG GUNG
30 Pell Street

MEN'S   ★★★★

NUMBER OF STALLS   2

NUMBER OF URINALS   2

NUMBER OF SINKS   2

CLEANLINESS RATING   EXCELLENT

AMENITIES: These people know their lavatories: excellent lighting, very beautiful decor (like a country club). Everything is new... the plumbing, the liquid soap, the extraordinarily soft toilet paper, the floors and walls. But no towels, just air-drying.

ACCESSIBILITY: Ask for directions: it's downstairs.

WHEELCHAIR ACCESS: NO

GENERAL COMMENTS: This restaurant recently opened. Its toilets are large, clean, and nearly perfect.

WOMEN'S ★★★★
NUMBER OF STALLS 4
NUMBER OF SINKS 3
CLEANLINESS RATING EXCELLENT

AMENITIES: On par with the best: excellent lighting, modern, attractive decor, with a huge mirror to catch and return your satisfied reflection. Bar soap, which is okay, but no towels... only machines to air dry your hands. The quality of the toilet paper is good.

ACCESSIBILITY: It's downstairs.

WHEELCHAIR ACCESS: NO

GENERAL COMMENTS: Pleasant, clean and very big. The management should be proud of this place. So should the N.Y. health department people.

MARY FLOWER TEA PARLOR
76 Mott Street

WOMEN'S ★
NUMBER OF STALLS 1

NUMBER OF SINKS   1
CLEANLINESS RATING   POOR

AMENITIES: This is a medieval toilet. The plumbing is bad, the mirror is small, and there is no soap. However, you'll find paper towels and normal toilet paper.

ACCESSIBILITY: Back of the restaurant

WHEELCHAIR ACCESS: NO

GENERAL COMMENTS: Not very clean, and the smell is (ahem) unpleasant.

AREA G: WALL STREET

POINTS OF INTEREST

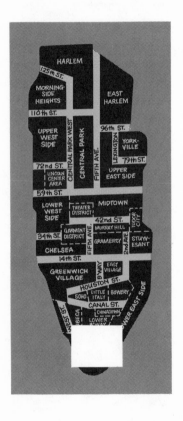

1. **FULTON FISH MARKET** A great place to start off the morning's walk. Take a deep breath and see what we mean.

2. **SOUTH STREET SEAPORT** Terrific tourist place, and a fascinating nautical museum. Lots of shops, too.

3. **ST. PAUL'S CHAPEL** The oldest church in town. Old churchyard, too. Ask to see George Washington's pew.

4. **WORLD TRADE CENTER** Two very tall buildings with too many people all calling the elevator at once.

5. **AMERICAN STOCK EXCHANGE** Not as big as the New York Stock Exchange, but no less interesting.

6. TRINITY CHURCH
Known by the cemetery it keeps, and some very beautiful stained glass windows. Quiet and pleasant.

7. NEW YORK STOCK EXCHANGE
This is the noisy one you always see on the business news channel.

8. FRAUNCES TAVERN
You probably remember it as the Queen's Head (1762). George Washington drank here.

Some of these points of interest are covered in greater detail on the following pages, together with detailed toilet reports. Please note that, just beneath Fulton Street is John Street, which we regard as a favorable omen.

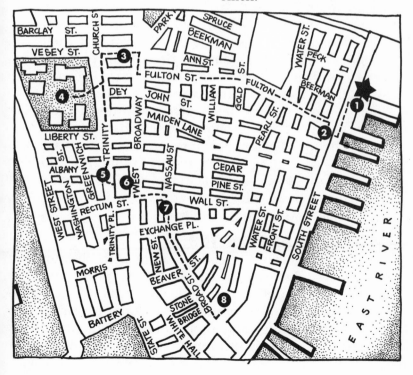

NEW YORK STOCK EXCHANGE

One way to financial security is to own the sweep-up concession at the New York Stock Exchange. It is estimated that, at the end of a typical business day, more than two tons of crumpled paper lie on the floor of the Exchange. These scraps represent the dreams, aspirations, frustrations, and shattered futures of millions of tiny investors nationwide. They also represent the prudent strategies of insiders, major institutions, and Wall Street Journal reporters. Following the Revolutionary War, the First Continental Congress learned their new nation was about $80 million in debt, so they issued stock to offset the war bills. But traders complained the procedure was too disorganized, so to correct the situation, 24 of them met every nice day under a sycamore tree to conduct their business. That tree stood on the site of the current building, a Greek revivalist structure. On weekdays, tourists can crowd into the second-floor visitors gallery, tears streaming down their faces, to watch their life savings dissolve into scrap heaps. Former brokers and arbitrageurs, guilty of poor judgment, now act as guides and are available to answer questions, although few of them have been told the precise location of the Exchange's public toilet facilities.

WORLD TRADE CENTER

Architects, working in collaboration with elevator engineers, decided that a 220-story glass and steel tower would be impractical on this five-acre site; elevator cables would be too long, requiring excessive splicing, and their sheer weight might be budged only if immense roof motors were installed, and that would be unsightly for airline passengers. So the floor plans were simply bisected and two 110-story towers were constructed instead. Fifty thousand people go to work in these buildings every day, many with nosebleeds and oxygen tanks. How many remain industrious for a full seven or eight hours is difficult to ascertain because of all the external distractions, and also because still another 80,000 people visit the twin towers to conduct business, ride the elevators, bump into others in the corridors, or merely to gape out of the Windows On The World, an extraordinary restaurant perched on the 107th floor, offering high-altitude, high-priced food and an unduplicatable view. `Way downstairs are a subterranean car park that can precipitate a 2000-vehicle gridlock, several other less elaborate restaurants and bars, a subway station, and a shopping concourse for those who would rather buy than eat. If stratospheric buildings excite you, The World Trade Center offers a double dose.

TRINITY CHURCH

Historians with tenure agree that a cemetery is known by the people it keeps. And so it is with the churchyard that surrounds Trinity Church on three sides. It's no fun going through a modern cemetery, with few celebrities' names on the tombstones, but you don't have to be Christian to appreciate a walk among the dead and famous at Trinity Church. Alexander Hamilton is buried here (our first Secretary of the Treasury and a signatory of the Declaration of Independence), and Robert Fulton, who gave up a promising career as a portrait artist to concentrate on steam engines. The plots thicken. Indeed, their history goes back to 1681, nearly 40 years before the first Trinity Church was erected. That one burned down in 1776, and its successor was torn down in 1839, to be replaced by the one that stands here today, designed by English architect Richard Upjohn, with bronze doors by Richard Morris. After some tricky politicking, the Church was permitted to keep its vast land holdings (granted by Queen Anne) after the Revolution, and, by exercising its rights as a major New York landlord, it no longer has to depend on passing a collection plate for its survival, or getting written into the wills of aging parishioners.

*Following: Some Toilets
in the Neighborhood*

NEW YORK STOCK EXCHANGE Visitors Center
20 Broad Street

MEN'S ★★★

NUMBER OF STALLS	5
NUMBER OF URINALS	3
NUMBER OF SINKS	3
CLEANLINESS RATING	FAIR

AMENITIES: Big dividends in lighting and plumbing, but a depressed state insofar as decor is concerned: dingy yellow tile, odd-smelling liquid soap and only one hand dryer. But look for reasonably good returns in fine, single-ply toilet paper and quality paper toweling. A sickly-sweet, deodorized aroma pervades this busy room, evidence of some sort of coverup, perhaps?

ACCESSIBILITY: Fairly easy to find although the

exchange itself is confusing; perhaps a better ventilating system would help, or less hectic patrons.

WHEELCHAIR ACCESS: YES

GENERAL COMMENTS: It's free, but you must wait to use it.

WOMEN'S ★★★

NUMBER OF STALLS	3
NUMBER OF SINKS	3
CLEANLINESS RATING	FAIR

AMENITIES: The trash containers are oversubscribed, and the pink, orange and grey decor is not too attractive, but the fluorescent lighting and plumbing are okay (if you're prepared for an explosive flush). Nice paper towels on a roll, liquid soap, and a Tampax machine, but research indicates no table or makeup ledge anywhere.

ACCESSIBILITY: You'll have to get a key from the checkperson, and only two out of the three toilets worked.

WHEELCHAIR ACCESS: YES

GENERAL COMMENTS: Hot, overcrowded, small and too many scraps of paper on the floor (just like the Exchange).

FEDERAL RESERVE BUILDING
33 W. Liberty Street

MEN'S ★★★★

NUMBER OF STALLS	5
NUMBER OF URINALS	5
NUMBER OF SINKS	6
CLEANLINESS RATING	EXCELLENT

AMENITIES: The Feds know how to treat the citizenry; perfect natural lighting from stained glass windows, and lots of bright, fluorescent tubes. Beautiful marble-slab stalls, automatic shut-off sinks, liquid soap, and well-stocked with good paper towels.

ACCESSIBILITY: You must sign in, receive a visitors badge, and pass a metal detector test. The guards practically conduct you to the bathroom. It's on the main floor.

WHEELCHAIR ACCESS: NO

GENERAL COMMENTS: There's practically nothing else worthwhile seeing in this edifice.

WOMEN'S ★★★★

NUMBER OF STALLS	7
NUMBER OF SINKS	4
CLEANLINESS RATING	EXCELLENT

AMENITIES: No odor, dirt, or trash. Unfortunately the choice of fluorescent color makes one's skin look green in the mirrors. Bright white tile, grey marble suspended between the stalls, excellent plumbing. A useless pink liquid soap is available, as are thick, white paper towels.

ACCESSIBILITY: Like boarding a plane in the Middle East; you'll need to get a visitors pass and have everything metal-detected.

WHEELCHAIR ACCESS: YES
Through the employees' entrance

GENERAL COMMENTS: Superior, spacious, sterile, slick, serviceable.

TRINITY CHURCH
Broadway at Wall

MEN'S   ★★★

NUMBER OF STALLS   2
NUMBER OF URINALS   2
NUMBER OF SINKS   2
CLEANLINESS RATING   EXCELLENT

AMENITIES: Quiet, serenely tiled walls and a floor that is clean and pure. Pleasant incandescent light under a 15-foot-high, freshly-painted ceiling, with a pretty stained glass window on one wall. Functional plumbing, and one each liquid soap dispenser and paper towel dispenser.

ACCESSIBILITY: On the main floor toward the back.

WHEELCHAIR ACCESS: YES
But there are steps up from street.

GENERAL COMMENTS: We leave it to the theologians: Is it blasphemous to put a church bathroom directly behind the altar?

WOMEN'S   ★★★★

NUMBER OF STALLS   2
NUMBER OF SINKS   2
CLEANLINESS RATING   EXCELLENT

AMENITIES: Well-lit, good mirrors and a ledge for your purse. Spirit-lifting white tile over yellow tile floors; good plumbing, liquid soap, and paper towels. There is a connecting lounge, but it has no mirror, is carpeted in brown, and has virtually no lighting. Not even a candle. It looks a little like a storeroom.

ACCESSIBILITY: Not obvious, no signs, but if you need to find it, it will be there.

WHEELCHAIR ACCESS: YES
Four steps up from the street, but after that the coast is clear.

GENERAL COMMENTS: Very nice, but would you expect anything less from a well-endowed church?

FEDERAL HALL
(Former Custom House/Treasury)
Corner Wall & Broad Sts.

MEN'S   ★★★

NUMBER OF STALLS	3
NUMBER OF URINALS	3
NUMBER OF SINKS	2
CLEANLINESS RATING	EXCELLENT

AMENITIES: Kept clean by Julio Rodriquez, with a sense of commitment. Bright lighting, insouciant, institutional green and white tile, with good plumbing, drip deodorizers, liquid soap, and well-stocked with paper towels.

ACCESSIBILITY: It's marked; you'll find it in the basement.

WHEELCHAIR ACCESS: YES
Use the elevator.

GENERAL COMMENTS: Functional and nondescript, but the 1842 hall itself could be a national monument. Maybe it is.

WOMEN'S ★★★

NUMBER OF STALLS   5

NUMBER OF SINKS   3

CLEANLINESS RATING   EXCELLENT

AMENITIES: Spotless. Good fluorescent lighting, but the tile is boring. Very good plumbing, sinks are the kind that don't stay on, and the mirrors are over a four-inch ledge. Liquid soap, brown paper towels, and a Tampax machine that was out of order.

ACCESSIBILITY: It's in the basement, with a small sign on the main floor. You can use the elevator or stairs.

WHEELCHAIR ACCESS: YES

GENERAL COMMENTS: Maybe too much flowery deodorant, but that's a more acceptable alternative.

McDONALD'S
160 Broadway

MEN'S ★★★

NUMBER OF STALLS   1

NUMBER OF URINALS   1

NUMBER OF SINKS   1

CLEANLINESS RATING   GOOD

AMENITIES: Lighting may be a little too green, but there's nice, earth-tone tile, and the plumbing and timed faucets are new, and properly programmed for a decent rinse. Liquid soap, electric air-dry machines. Truly a McToilet for the nineties.

ACCESSIBILITY: Right on the main floor, easy to find. Fast food management obviously recognizes the importance of good sanitary facilities to attract hungry patrons.

WHEELCHAIR ACCESS: YES

GENERAL COMMENTS: An exceptional toilet for such a high volume restaurant. Someone responsible for keeping this place clean and well-stocked must be well-motivated. He takes his job seriously.

WOMEN'S ★★★

NUMBER OF STALLS	2
NUMBER OF SINKS	1
CLEANLINESS RATING	GOOD

AMENITIES: Smells like fries, but otherwise far better than you'd expect. Fluorescent lighting, pink and grey tiles, white plumbing, green liquid soap, and chrome hand-dryers. Biodegradable toilet tissue. Hooks for coats and trash containers are in each stall, and there's a good mirror for those who wish to freshen up before rejoining their dinner guests in the main hall.

ACCESSIBILITY: Right in front, on the main floor.

WHEELCHAIR ACCESS: YES
One stall is equipped with handrails and a raised seat.

GENERAL COMMENTS: Perfectly serviceable, and unusually clean when you consider several thousand people must pass through these portals each day.

FULTON MARKET South Street Seaport
Fulton and Water Streets

MEN'S ★★★

NUMBER OF STALLS	10
NUMBER OF URINALS	11
NUMBER OF SINKS	10
CLEANLINESS RATING	FAIR

AMENITIES: Your basic white with pleasant, dirt-obscuring brown tile floors, all ensconced in a building that boasts new plumbing in good condition. There is liquid soap at each sink, the lighting is adequate, and three air dryers stand ready to blow hotly all over your palms and fingers.

ACCESSIBILITY: On the mezzanine, with signs at the entrance.

WHEELCHAIR ACCESS: YES
Use the elevator; there are separate wheelchair facilities.

GENERAL COMMENTS: Well-kept, but spartan, with lots of deodorizers.

WOMEN'S ★★★

NUMBER OF STALLS	17
NUMBER OF SINKS	10
CLEANLINESS RATING	GOOD

AMENITIES: This is a huge, well-lit facility with exposed pipes that make you feel like you're aboard ship. White cinderblock walls, brown tile floor, and a reasonably clean mirror over every sink. One long table, also fitted with a mirror, and

Alfreda Ofal is the moniker one of our trusted toilet researchers uses when a shortage of female investigators forces him to assume a disguise to inspect and grade women's lavatories. It is a commentary on the New York mentality that for weeks, "Alfreda" plied her trade undetected even though many persons would concede that the masquerade is not totally convincing. When she *was* discovered it was by a policeman in a hooker's disguise, prowling the ladies' room of a fancy hotel. Alfreda was arrested and taken down to the precinct station, where authorities agreed to drop the charges if Mr. Ofal would simply forget the whole incident, as well as the number of the arresting officer's shield.

liquid soap with machines that blow hot air on your hands with nearly indiscernible effect. Nice toilet paper.

ACCESSIBILITY: On the mezzanine, and well-marked as you enter the building.

WHEELCHAIR ACCESS: YES
There is a specially equipped wheelchair bathroom with one toilet, a sink, and air-dry blower.

GENERAL COMMENTS: Have no reservations about a visit to this Fulton facility. Children welcome.

CHAPTER 5:
WE STAND
TOGETHER

In a world of impoverished toilets, man and womankind need relief. In vain we cry out for more public toilets, bigger public toilets, and easier access to them. What we need are enlightened architects, engineers, developers and urban planners, not anal-retentive louts and their sluggish minions.

Working as individuals there is little we can do to alter existing conditions. But, acting together, we can influence the people in power and make them sit up and take notice of our collective plight.

As a group we could hire a lobbyist in Washington and perhaps another at the U.N. (where their *own* facilities could use some attention.) Women in particular could demand more commodes, more space for queuing up, and an occasional shelf or two under the mirrors to rest pocketbooks or packages.

As a group, we could ask for more frequent cleaning inspections to insure dry floors, ample paper supplies, plumbing that works, and a light level that enables one to see his or her own knees without striking a match.

To enable us to achieve this strength in numbers we propose membership in an organization—a group of dedicated citizens who subscribe to the initiatives and benefits outlined above, and who are willing to throw themselves bodily into the foray.

The organization of which we speak is called, simply, *The Society to Help Improve Toilets.* Current membership is admittedly sparse. But if there were thousands of anxious, committed, concerned people, all eager to improve lavatory conditions, nothing could impede our progress. With S.H.I.T. behind us, we could walk into any mayor's office and demand to see the head of the planning commission, the head building inspector, or even the mayor himself.

We could send more letters to newspapers and radio stations, sensitizing the press to this deplorable situation. Crusading television network news shows would do documentaries... "Inside Toilets, U.S.A." We could storm magazines like *Time* and *Newsweek* and demand that they take up the battle. It would be pretty difficult for an editor to disregard a business card with S.H.I.T. on it.

Think of it...whether you're a man or woman, that is the power you could wield as a member in good standing or sitting.

The time to start is now. The accompanying membership form (or a photocopy of it) can be filled out and mailed with a check for $6.00 ($8.00 Canadian) made out to Ken Eichenbaum. In return you'll receive a membership card and a copy of the s.h.i.t. newsletter ("On A Roll") whenever we can get around to publishing it. Enroll a friend or relative and we guarantee they'll be astonished by what they get in the mail.

Will it be easy? No. Trying to get hotels and restaurants to open their facilities to non-dining, non-resident tourists will not be a simple task. Attempting to persuade the designer of a new museum or concert hall to install *adequate* plumbing is never easy. But working together—focusing our efforts as one giant s.h.i.t. organization—we can make the difference between success or failure. When we take our-uh-roll call, will your name be on it?

MEMBERSHIP APPLICATION FOR
THE SOCIETY TO HELP IMPROVE TOILETS

NAME_____

ADDRESS_____

_____ ZIP _____

OCCUPATION _____

YES! I wish to seek a civilized solution to the problem of public toilets both here and abroad. To this end, I pledge my strength, wisdom, and six bucks to help make toilets more accessible, more numerous, and better equipped. In particular I would work very diligently to dispense with all electric hot-air hand dryers, and rusty plungers that leak viscous green liquid detergent.

MY COMMITTEE PREFERENCES
(CHOOSE ANY THREE IN ORDER OF PREFERENCE)

☐ More and Bigger Toilets   ☐ Raunchy Interior Decor
☐ Cleanliness Inspections   ☐ Reading Materials
☐ Wheelchair Access   ☐ Speakers Bureau
☐ Softer Toilet Paper   ☐ Other (please describe)
☐ Disposable Seat Covers   _____

Please enclose check or money order for $6.00 ($8.00 Canadian) made out to Ken Eichenbaum. Mail to LITTERATI BOOKS, 4100 West River Lane, Milwaukee, WI USA 53209.

☐ This membership is for me. Put my name on the card.
☐ This is a gift membership. Enclose a note that says (10-12 words, please):_____

_____

☐ Mail membership card and a copy of *On A Roll*, if it ever gets published, to: ☐ Mr. ☐ Ms.

GIFTEE NAME ON
MEMBERSHIP CARD _____

ADDRESS: _____

_____ ZIP _____

Please allow 3 to 4 weeks for delivery, longer if it's going to Sri Lanka or Brisbane.

INDEX

For Emergency Use Only

For Emergency Use Only

For Emergency Use Only

For Emergency Use Only

For Emergency Use Only

LITTERATI BOOKS